Dr Viv Shackleton is a chartered occupational psychologist, researcher and a businessman as well as joint author of *Psychology and Work* (Methuen, 1975) and *Individual Differences* (Methuen, 1984).

A lecturer at Aston Business School, Aston University, Birmingham, he teaches undergraduates, postgraduates and managers and has held university appointments in the USA and continental Europe, as well as in Britain. His teaching and research specialisms are in employee selection and managerial assessment. Dr Shackleton is also an associate of Ashridge Management College, where he is a consultant and a member of the team running the Leadership Programme.

As a businessman, he is director of a consultancy firm. He advises companies on setting up employee recruitment and selection systems and on the management of people. His clients range from family businesses to multinationals.

Bob Garratt is a management consultant, Chairman of Media Projects International, and Visiting Fellow at the Management School of Imperial College, London. He is Chairman of the Association for Management Education and Development.

Other books for the Successful Manager series:

Information and Organisations, Max Boisot
Managing Your Own Career, Dave Francis
The Learning Organisation, Bob Garratt
Manage Your Time, Sally Garratt
Superteams: A Blueprint for Organisational Success, Colin Hastings et al
Roots of Excellence, Ronnie Lessem
The Eloquent Executive, William Parkhurst
Managing Yourself, Mike Pedler & Tom Boydell
Managing Change and Making It Stick, Roger Plant
Finance for the Perplexed Executive, Ray Proctor

Viv Shackleton

How to Pick People for Jobs

FONTANA/Collins

First published in 1989 by Fontana Paperbacks
8 Grafton Street, London W1X 3LA

Set in Linotron Times

Printed and bound in Great Britain by
William Collins Sons & Co. Ltd., Glasgow

Contents

Preface

What is this book about?

This book is about how to pick people to work with you. It looks at how to choose the right person for the job.

The book takes you along a path from deciding what sort of person you want, to making up your mind if you've found them. It will advise you on the interview. It'll give you insights into some good methods you can use apart from just the boring old standard interview. Mostly, I hope it will increase your chances of picking the right person.

I am clear what the book is not. It is not an academic tome, full of complicated research and turgid prose. It is practical and down-to-earth. It is not aimed at personnel specialists. Although I like to think they will find some parts novel and interesting, they know a lot of this stuff already. And it won't turn you into a selection professional overnight. It will, though, make your task of selecting people more straightforward.

Who is the book for?

I have an image of the person who will get most out of this book. It is you the manager, the entrepreneur, the business executive, the shopkeeper, the accountant, the quantity surveyor, the flower seller. Your may have professional qualifications to your name, or you may have learnt what you do in the school of hard knocks. No matter. What you have in common is that you have a skill. And you have people, or maybe just one person, working for you or with you. What you have little experience of is the crucial job of hiring people. This book is for you.

Filthy lucre

If you've got this far, and are still standing in the bookshop reading, do the honourable thing. Take out your money and buy this book. You won't regret it. Promise.

> 'Writing is the only profession where no one considers you ridiculous if you earn no money.'
>
> OSCAR WILDE

> 'Sir, no man but a blockhead ever wrote except for money.'
>
> SAMUEL JOHNSON

Acknowledgements

It is the tradition in books to thank everyone in sight. But I really do want to thank those people who helped me in the making of this book.

Friends and colleagues gave up their time to read, comment, and suggest improvements to early drafts. They are Neil Anderson, Brian Ellison, Clive Fletcher, Ian Glendon, Jane Hodgson, Sue Newell and Adrian Savage.

Mark Lawson of Helix Ltd kindly gave me permission to include Helix application forms in the book. Ivan Robertson of UMIST and Macmillan gave permission for application forms to be included from *The Theory and Practice of Systematic Staff Selection* (1986) by M. Smith and I. T. Robertson.

Most of all, I want to thank my wife. She proof-read drafts, advised on exercises, helped type, commented on my English and kept me sane. Thanks, Margaret.

Viv Shackleton
Aston Business School
Aston University
Birmingham

Note: A man and a woman

A word about the use of gender words in this book. I think that if you have to read 'she or he', 'his or hers' throughout a book it's a bore. Worse is '(s)he' or 's/he'. It's clumsy and gets in the way. But the principle of not just using male pronouns is important. What I have done is use female words in some chapters and male words in others, with roughly equal numbers throughout the book. So where you see 'she', please imagine you see 'she or he'; where you read 'his', read 'his or her'; and so on.

1 Why you Need to Get it Right

'Work is the refuge of people who have nothing better to do.'
Oscar Wilde

'Without work all life goes rotten.'
Albert Camus

This book is aimed at anyone who needs to employ someone.

If you are such a person, then you're not alone. For you, and for thousands like you, it is an important, difficult, time consuming and expensive task, fraught with problems and pitfalls to trap the novice or the unwary. Picking the right people means large potential gains in job satisfaction, productivity and time, for you and for those who work with you. Getting it wrong means expense, frustration, recriminations and headaches.

So why is it that so many of us recognize picking people for jobs as a problem? After all, much of our lives is spent meeting and talking to people and then making up our minds about them. Do we like them? Shall we have them round to dinner? Is he suitable to go out with our daughter? Can I trust this woman? Shall I vote for this politician or that one? Would I buy a used car from this man? And so on. These situations all involve us in meeting people, summing them up and making decisions about them. Picking people for jobs is no different. So why bother to write a book about it (in my case) or read it (in yours)?

The Price we Pay

One major cause of the hesitation, sometimes fear, we feel at selecting others is that it is very expensive to get it wrong. If you choose a television set and it blows up shortly after you buy it, you can always get your money back. If the people I become friends with on holiday turn out to be awful bores after the second day, I can always avoid them for the rest of the week. But if we make a mistake in selecting someone to work with us, undoing the mistake can be a lot more difficult. And costly.

A managing director told me recently about the time he hired a production manager who was not up to the job and left after a year. He calculated that the mistake had cost his company over £100,000.

So let's look at the costs of picking a wrong person.

Start-up costs

There are all the direct costs of recruitment. These include advertising, the selector's time, maybe a recruitment consultant's fees, the candidates' travelling expenses, and so on.

Lost pay . . .

There are the wages you paid them when they were with you, while getting little effective work from them in return.

. . . And benefits

As you may know only too well, there are also the costs of all the extras that go with hiring someone. It isn't just the wage bill. This is only around half the true amount. There are National Insurance payments, office running costs, pensions benefits, and so on. Take the salary and double it, to get a rough picture of the true figure. It is often more than this for managers and professionals, and much more for the expensive London or southeast areas of Britain.

Rank Xerox were very concerned about the expense of employing their managers and professionals at the London head office, so the Xanadu project was conceived. This involved encouraging a number of staff to resign as full-time employees of the company and work as freelance consultants from home. Rank Xerox gave them computers and electronic means of communicating with head office and with each other on favourable financial terms. It also guaranteed a certain amount of work for the first few years. As a result, it waved goodbye to an outlay per employee of over £50,000 just to have them occupy central London offices.

Your loss, someone else's gain

The waste of your time and theirs in training someone, only to see them go and use their new skills with another employer. The first few years spent by a graduate in his first job can cost the employer between £10,000 and £15,000 in *formal* training, let alone informal training.

If only you'd got it right

Then there are what economists call the 'opportunity costs'. This is the amount of money the business might have made if the new employee had lived up to expectations. Plus the amount of business lost because you had to wait weeks, months, or even years, to find a replacement.

Bad apples

There may be costs associated with those who remain, the 'bad apple' syndrome. You probably recognize from your own experience that high labour turnover can make those who remain question their own reasons for staying. It can decrease their motivation and job satisfaction and increase the chances that they will look round for another job. 'After all,' they may say to themselves, 'if Mary has decided to go, perhaps the job isn't worth me hanging around for either.'

The disgruntled employee

All this ignores the considerable cost to the employee himself. There is the job dissatisfaction, the wasted time, the aggro and the frustration of starting a job which he then leaves. He may also have blotted his copybook for the next time. Future potential employers may look unfavourably on someone who can only hold down a job for six months.

It may not be the candidate's fault he was unsuitable. It might have been poor selection. Or shoddy selection may reflect a deeper malaise in the organization. But the leaver may have a hard job convincing the next interviewer of that.

Adding it all up

Putting a total figure on it is not easy. I'll bet, though, that if you or your accountant add it up properly, you can double the amount you first thought of.

A study of graduates in their first job, who left within a year, showed that it cost their employers three times their first year's salary. At the present time, this means that just one poor graduate selection decision can cost an employer around £30,000.

For most jobs, the direct and indirect costs of making a wrong decision are generally reckoned to be equivalent to at least two years' salary for the job.

This book may save you the price you paid for it a thousand times over!

What to Do if you Make a Mess of It

So what are the options if you do get it wrong and select an unsuitable person for the job? Are you stuck with them?

1. One point to note is that in reality there are shades of 'right' and 'wrong', good and bad, candidates. Even the best recruit will have weaknesses. Even the worst is likely to have some ability which can be developed.

So a good alternative is to train and develop the person in the job. This has many potential advantages. It may lead to greater commitment from the employee. It can lead to greater skill and flexibility in the workforce and have spin-offs for others who are trained at the same time. You will need to provide training even for suitable applicants as an on-going process.

Yet training means spending money. There are the direct costs of training staff time. And indirect, in the time the employee is being trained up and not doing the job for which he is paid.

2. You can get rid of them by sacking them or asking them to leave of their own accord. Legally, this is relatively easy up to six months after you have taken them on. You will incur the expense of selection all over again, but this may be less than keeping unsuitable people on.

3. Another alternative is to live with the decision. You may decide that the new employee is not exactly right, but you can put up with him. This is a strategy that keeps the immediate costs of replacement low, but increases the potential loss over the long term. In particular, the opportunity costs of not having someone who is ideally suited to the job increase as time goes by. And a dissatisfied worker, who knows that the job is OK but not ideal, can sour working relations for the whole of the rest of the team or department.

Right First Time

All in all, it is obviously better to get it right first time and employ someone who will do the job well. Getting good people in place is only part of the business of running an effective organization. But it is a very important part. So let's look at some of the things you need to do.

What should I do?

1. *Get some practice*
Practice helps us feel confident about selecting people. I have spent many years selecting and advising companies on selection, as well as teaching the techniques. I do it scores of times a year.

For you, the busy manager, this is usually not so. Selecting people is just one of a multitude of tasks you have to do. You probably only do it once or twice a year, if that. So, from talking to people like yourself, I know that one reason why you find picking people for jobs difficult is the unfamiliarity of the exercise.

It's lack of direct experience that's the problem. Most people who work have been on the receiving end of recruitment and selection. I'm sure you are no exception. You've filled in application forms, been interviewed, and maybe even been given employment tests or samples of the job to do before being taken on. Yet you've probably rarely been on the other side of the fence. Rarely have you had to get your hands dirty and get down to choosing someone who can do a job of work for you, can fit in with the organization, can get on with the others who already work there (won't offend anyone may be nearer the mark!) and generally earn their pay and a bit more besides.

The problem has been made worse in recent years by the decline of the Personnel Department in many organizations. Once upon a time most organizations had personnel departments who could be relied upon to at least help with selection. Now more and more companies leave selection totally to the line manager. This may be no bad thing. After all, it's usually the manager who has to work with the new person. But they are often untrained and unprepared for selection.

2. *Get some training*

Better than untutored experience is training. Just about every organization I know lets untrained managers interview. Yet these same companies wouldn't allow people to do other jobs without some instruction. They wouldn't let inexperienced managers play the money markets, for example, or prepare the accounts. They also agonize over capital expenditure decisions such as computer systems or the company car fleet. Yet people are the most vital resource an organization has. The same care and experience is needed here as in other parts of the business.

3. *Read this book*

So the problem is one of unfamiliarity; of how to go about the job of picking the right people when you have only a vague idea of how to go about it. I hope in this book to make the unfamiliar become a little more well-known; to make the amateur selector a little more professional.

From Baby Boom to Baby Bust

As if the price of getting it wrong weren't bad enough, it's going to get more difficult to find replacements. In the 1990s, we are all going to find it harder and harder to locate the labour to recruit, especially graduates, executives and professionals.

The shrinking number of school leavers

For one thing, there will soon be a massive decline in the number of school leavers. Department of Education and Science statistics show that since 1970 the birth rate in the UK has dropped considerably.

LIVE BIRTHS IN THE UK

Year of Birth	*Live Births (thousands)*	*16 Years on (school-leaving age)*
1955	789	1971
1960	918	1976
1965	997	1981
1970	904	1986
1975	698	1991
1980	753	1996

The table shows that sixteen- to eighteen-year-old school leavers will fall to a very low number between 1991 and 1996. The stark fact is that if children aren't born they can't leave school!

The Department of Education's figures suggest that only around 804,400 pupils left school in 1988, down 36,000 compared with the previous year. Forecasts show the figure dropping to 680,000 by 1991. From 1987 to 1994 the youth labour market will have declined by 25%. A Confederation of British Industry (CBI) report warns that the area most harshly affected will be in the fewer than five

O-levels group. Between 1987 and 1995, those leaving school with A-levels will fall about 19%, but for those with fewer than the equivalent of five O-levels the drop will be 22%.

So the competition for school leavers is going to be hot. Moreover, twenty large employers, including the NHS, the Civil Service and Banks, Building Societies and other financial service organizations take on around half of all school leavers at the present time. For example, the big banks between them take on some 20,000 school leavers each year. If large employers like these maintain or raise their overall numbers in the next few years, it leaves precious few left over for smaller firms.

A lot of big employers are not standing still. Many are worried and are taking active steps to hold on to their share of school leavers. They have the money to do it. The Department of Health normally takes on some 20,000 a year from school. In 1988 it spent £2.5m on a recruitment campaign including advertisements on television.

Even popular employers are having trouble finding people. The hairdressers, Vidal Sassoon, used to have teenage girls queuing outside its West End head office for a chance to enrol on the salon's training course. In 1988 the hairdressing company had to advertise for the first time to attract new entrants. It is also offering extra inducements including higher wages as well as clothes and travel allowances.

A declining number of graduates

If we turn to graduates, the picture is just as bleak. First, more and more employers are taking on people with degrees. This is not just in the usual occupations such as the professions (law, medicine, accountancy, etc), research, management and administration, but also 'new' employers of graduates in such growth areas as retailing. Second, this expansion is happening at a time when the supply of new graduates has stopped growing. This is a result of the declining number of school leavers and government policy to cut back the funding of higher education. In 1988 British universities and polytechnics produced just 1,000 computer science graduates, for example.

The Institute of Manpower Studies predicts that the demand for graduates will grow over the coming years, especially in mechanical engineering, chemistry, high technology, information technology and teaching.

Shortages are already with us. In 1988 the Institute reported that half of all graduate recruiters had unfilled vacancies.

Just as with school leavers, the small employer is going to have a rough time attracting graduates. The big, prestigious employers take so many. Accountancy as a whole takes 5,000 (with one firm, Peat, Marwick, McLintock, taking around 1,000), the Civil Service takes around 4,000 and GEC/Marconi another 1,000. It is predicted that professional groups are going to increase their intake massively from now until 1995.

Fewer people, more pay

It is obvious what this all means for you, if you want to recruit graduates. It means lots of competition, and it means you'll have to pay higher starting salaries. It's already happening. In 1982 the average starting salary for a graduate was around 66% of the average male earnings. By 1988 it was 80%, or around £9,000.

You may be able to think of other sources of manpower you could tap to offset the shortage of school leavers and graduates. Part-time workers, often mothers of young children, is one source. The long-term unemployed or retired people are others. But this will demand new and more careful recruitment and selection methods.

Banks have been particularly active in tempting women back to work, often as part-timers, and are offering increasingly attractive terms. The main lure is a cheap mortgage but nurseries and profit-sharing schemes are multiplying. Yet it is a privileged minority of employers who can offer such perks. Not many can offer low interest mortgages, for example.

So, it's not a very optimistic picture for those of you trying to recruit and select employees. This makes it even more important to do a good job of systematically recruiting and selecting suitable people. Let's look at how to go about it.

Key Points

1. Wrong selection decisions are very expensive. There are both direct and indirect costs.

2. It is going to get harder to find the labour to recruit.

    - The number of school leavers is declining
    - Graduates are not getting any more plentiful, and there are many more employers looking to take them on. They are also getting pricier; starting salaries for graduates are going up faster than average earnings

3. This puts a premium on careful and systematic recruitment and selection.

4. Picking the right people for the job has pay-offs for both employers and employees.

2 What is the Job Like?

'I think that maybe in every company today there is always at least one person who is going crazy slowly.'

Joseph Heller

'There are an enormous number of managers who have retired on the job.'

Peter Drucker

Recruiting for the Company

You need to recruit a person to your organization. Where do you start?

Do you REALLY need someone?

The best place to start is to consider whether you really need that person at all. It is easy to jump to the conclusion that if someone leaves, you must take on someone else to replace them. This is certainly not the case. In view of the costs pointed out in Chapter 1, it is worth your considering in some depth whether the job needs filling at all. Let's look at some alternatives. You could:

- Subcontract the work
- Rearrange the hours
- Reorganize the work
- Give the job to a machine

1. *Subcontract the work*
If you pay someone to do the work who is not a direct employee, you avoid the costs of employing people in the slack periods when

there's no work for them to do. Subcontracting is becoming more and more common. Probably your own organization does it. Local authorities are subcontracting the cleaning of schools and hospitals to contract cleaning companies. Personnel departments contract out the advertising and shortlisting of applicants for vacancies to recruitment agencies. Many businesses subcontract computer programming to firms such as F International, the very successful company which employs large numbers of mainly female programmers and analysts based at home. What you lose in loss of direct control of these employeess you gain in flexibility. You can decide to buy their services or not, as the need arises. You have the control that comes from paying them piece by piece for the work they do.

2. *Rearrange the hours*

Another possibility is to use overtime. Extra hours for those who already have jobs may seem unfair in times of high unemployment, but it is popular with employers, particularly for coping with a short term problem.

Alternatively you could make the job part-time. This is becoming increasingly popular, particularly among women workers. It also holds out the possibility of extending it to two part-time jobs (a job share) at a later stage.

3. *Reorganize the work*

Perhaps you could spread out the work among the existing workforce. You might be able to persuade the particular department or team which has the vacancy to absorb the work along with their own. Or someone from another department with little to do, or whose job is redundant, could be given the job, perhaps with some retraining.

4. *Give the job to a machine*

There is often scope for the work to be automated, or given to a computer. Some years ago, the Dean of a University Business School made the decision to supply every member of staff with a personal computer. This allowed them to write memos, letters, books, research papers, and deal with all the other necessary paperwork without the need for so many secretaries. I know of a factory that has recently cut its labour force by a third by introducing 'pick and place' robots. To know whether it makes economic sense to replace people with machines requires careful consideration of the relative sums involved. But it's often possible.

So the first step is to pause and think carefully whether you really need another body around the work place.

How to decide what you're looking for

When you have considered these other options and decided that, after all, you do need someone, what next? There is an old expression: if you don't know where you're going, you'll end up somewhere else. This is never more true than in picking people for jobs. The most important first requirement is to decide what sort of person you require. There are three major steps in this process.

JOB ANALYSIS
JOB DESCRIPTION
PERSON SPECIFICATION

Job Analysis

What is it?

Job analysis is the process of collecting and then analysing information about a job. This information includes the context in which the job is performed and the tasks and responsibilities involved. This gives you the basis for the job description, which we will come to in a minute.

For the purposes of this book, it is not important that I go into a great deal of detail about how to conduct a job analysis. It is a specialized activity, which has many purposes apart from personnel selection. These purposes include equal opportunities, restructuring a job, training, salary administration and productivity bargaining, to mention just a few.

The truth of the matter is that many selectors ignore job analysis altogether. They move straight to the job description. You do so at your peril, though. Job analysis is the foundation stone of successful staff selection. Without it, you, the selector, cannot know what you are aiming for when assessing candidates. It is like shooting in the dark.

Methods of job analysis

There are four major methods for analysing jobs. These are:

- Interviewing
- Questionnaires
- Observation
- Diaries

Interviewing and questionnaires are the most popular methods.

1. *Interviewing*
Interviewing in order to analyse the job should not be confused with interviewing candidates. Here the interview is conducted with present employees. It is designed to find out about the nature of the work so that we know what the *new* candidate will have to do.

2. *Questionnaires*
Again, these are used here to find out about the job, not to select applicants. Employees describe their jobs by answering a series of questions about what tasks or activities they do, how often they do them, how important they are, and so on.

3. *Observation*
Workers are observed as they carry out their job. Sometimes they are filmed. Information is recorded and analysed about the types of activity they perform.

4. *Diaries*
Here employees record their own activities in a work diary or log book. The analyst then uses the diaries to learn about the nature of the work.

The information obtained

A host of data can be gleaned from whichever job analysis method is used. This should include:

1. *Job features*
Job title
Main duties
Easy and difficult tasks
Pleasant and unpleasant tasks
Job context
The physical and social aspects of the workplace
How performance is measured

2. *People requirements*
Lots of information about the kind of people most capable of performing the job, including:
Abilities
Aptitudes
Physical requirements
Personality
Interests

All this is grist for the mill of job descriptions and person specifications.

Job Descriptions

Once a job analysis has been carried out, a job description can be written.

What are they?

As the name suggests, a job description is a report or document containing information which describes a job. The job may just have one person doing it, such as the one chief accountant in a firm. Or it might describe the job of a number of different people who all do the same job, such as the job of bus driver in a bus company. No matter. It is the job, not the person, which the text describes.

What use are they?

Most organizations of any size keep job descriptions. Yet these summaries are often ignored by employees as irrelevant. People just get on with the job as they see it. Robert Townsend, a former chief executive of Avis Car Rental, reckons that job descriptions are useless for a senior position. Executives shouldn't be tied down by these simple outlines, he says.

But job descriptions have many purposes. Their most common function is to help in job evaluation. This is where the job is assessed to decide on the pay a job holder should earn. Other uses can be seen in Figure. 2.1.

In 1984, Lesley Mackay and Derek Torrington at the University of Manchester Institute of Science and Technology (UMIST) conducted a questionnaire survey of personnel practice in 350 establishments in England, Scotland and Wales. It was reported in a book titled *The Changing Nature of Personnel Management*, published by the Institute of Personnel Management in 1986. Figure 2.1 opposite is adapted from that survey.

For you, the selector, the job description is a crucial document and an invaluable first step in the selection process. It sets out what the job entails and so gives clues as to what sort of person would be suitable for the job. Most personnel departments keep job descriptions of all the jobs in the company. Ask them for a copy. If you don't have a personnel department, or they don't keep job descriptions, you will have to ask the job holder to write one. You will find a section in this chapter on what information a job description should contain, and full examples both in this chapter and in Chapter 4.

Once you have got hold of a copy, you may find a snag. Job descriptions are often poorly constructed and out of date. So you may have to modify the document. Even so, at least you are not having to start from scratch.

It is not only selectors who find job descriptions useful. It is also candidates. It is always a good idea to send a copy to each

Question: List your three main uses of job descriptions.

Uses	Total of establishments quoting this use	Percentage of total of 350 establishments
Job evaluation/salary structure/upgrading/payment administration	243	69
Recruitment and selection	160	46
Organization structure/ review/planning/change/job development	94	27
Organization and methods/ staffing levels	87	24
Appraisal/assessment/ promotion	82	23
Training and development	80	23
To show the individual their role in the organization/ induction	40	11
Discipline and grievance	13	4

Figure 2.1: Torrington table

candidate at an early stage in the recruitment process. They need to know what the job involves just as much as you do. Then they can see if it fits their skills, experience, preferences and ambitions. If they see from the document that the job is not for them, you have saved a lot of your time as well as theirs. Not to mention the disappointment and frustration all round if the candidate only found out that the job didn't suit when it was too late – after having started it. Job descriptions help prevent this.

What does a job description look like?

Those of you who have already come across job descriptions will know that their form, content and length vary considerably according to the purpose for which they were written and the nature of the job. A reasonable job description should have the following features:

Job title
Main purpose of the job
Position in the organization
  Who the job holder reports to
  Who reports to the job holder
Key tasks or results areas.
  Scope of the job
  Limits of authority
Performance standards
Any other information

Figure 2.2 shows a typical job description for the job of personnel assistant. Have a look at it now.

JOB DESCRIPTION Puddlesea Metropolitan Borough
Personnel and Estates Department

POST TITLE Personnel Assistant

DEPT Personnel and Estates

SECTION Personnel

GRADE OF POST Scale 5/HS Hours 37 hours

PURPOSE OF THE JOB To assist in running the personnel function in the Authority.
To take part in the development of the service.

RELATIONSHIP TO OTHER POSTS WITHIN DEPARTMENT
Supervision given to: Nil
Supervision received from: Senior Personnel Officers
Personnel Officers
Training/Equal Opportunities Officer

KEY TASKS (*In order of priority*)
1. Under the supervision of the Assistant Director and Personnel Officers, to assist in the development and maintenance of the personnel functions. To undertake any ad hoc tasks or projects as delegated.
2. To carry out research as required to produce and interpret statistical data.
3. To provide back-up assistance as necessary to the Personnel and Welfare Services Section.
4. To provide asistance as necessary to the Training and Equal Opportunities Section.
5. To assist as required in problems arising from the administration of the Personnel Department.
6. To undertake such other duties as may arise from time to time.

CONTACTS

Daily: Director of Personnel and Estates; Assistant Director; Personnel Officers; Training Officer; Management staff in other departments.

Occasionally: Chief officers; Staff representatives of outside bodies.

EXPERIENCE, EDUCATION, SPECIAL QUALIFICATIONS AND TRAINING REQUIREMENTS The holder of the post should be a Member of the Institute of Personnel Management. Exceptionally the post may be filled by a trainee of graduate or equivalent status, who is prepared to study for the examinations of the Institute of Personnel Management.

The Assistant should have had related experience and have a sound knowledge of the personnel function.

CONTROL OF RESOURCES (HUMAN, FINANCIAL, MATERIAL) Nil

	DATE	INITIALS
PREPARED	1 January 1989	VJS
REVIEWED/CHECKED	3 January 1989	MC/HS
REVIEWED		

Figure 2.2: Typical job description for personnel assistant

On my desk at the moment are three job descriptions for different jobs in different companies, and none conforms to the ideal, textbook model. One is for the job of estates manager (someone who manages property) in a large chemical company, another for a marketing manager of a plastics company and another for a cost accountant with a giftware company. They are rather different, as you can see.

Estates manager	*Marketing Manager*	*Cost Accountant*
Job title	Job title	Job title
Operating group		Department
Position in organization	Reporting structure	Reports to
Summary of job	Purpose of job	Overview of job
Main tasks	Duties and responsibilities	Principal duties
Occasional duties		
Education		
Relationships		Resources
Discretion	Extent of authority	Extent of authority
Supervisory responsibilities		
Influence on results		
Creative work		
Working environment		
Additional information		
		Job holder
		Date compiled

What is important is not that these job descriptions *seem* different from each other or from a set standard. Just because the headings are different isn't, in itself, important. What is crucial is that the content fully outlines the job. I find the headings on my 'textbook' list a great help in this. But the acid test is whether or not the document can be used to draw up a person (or personnel) specification.

Person Specification

What is it?

The next stage is to decide what sort of person you are looking for. The job description tells us what the job holder does, or is expected to do. The person specification puts the job in 'people' terms; it tells you what are the main characteristics of successful job holders; it tells you what you are looking for. Then you know what qualities to assess in candidates.

The essence of effective selection is to match the job to be performed (described in the job description) with the profile of the person whom you need to do it successfully (described in the person specification).

The job to be done –	The profile of the person needed to do the job successfully –
described in the job description	described in the person specification

Figure 2.3: Matching the job to the person

How do I put one together?

There are a number of ways of deciding what characteristics go to make a successful employee in a particular job in your organization. Some methods are do-it-yourself. Others need some consultancy help. They include:

- Off-the-shelf plans
- Comparison of good and bad performers
- Critical incidents
- Repertory grid

Let's look at each in turn.

1. *Off-the-shelf plans*
The easiest way, though not the most effective, is to use one of the common, 'off-the-shelf' frameworks or plans. You have to construct the detail yourself, according to the job you are selecting for, but they give you headings to structure your thinking. The best known arc Monroe Frazer Five Fold Framework, the Alec Rodger Seven-Point Plan or the Eight-Point Plan.

PLANS

Five-point	*Seven-point*	*Eight-point*
Impact on people	Physical characteristics	
Qualifications	Attainments	
Brains and abilities	Intelligence	As 7-point
Motivation	Aptitudes	but with
Adjustment	Interests	addition of
	Disposition	Motivation
	Circumstance	

Figure 2.4 shows an eight-point plan person specification for a secretary.

These plans help structure your thoughts about the kind of person required for the job, and are simple and easy to draw up. They aren't intended to be interview questions, though. The frameworks give only limited help in guiding you on what to ask about in the interview.

Person specifications are not new. A type of ten-point plan for a chaplain, dating from 1665, is shown in Figure 2.5.

2. *Comparison of good and bad performers*
One way is to get together a number of people who know the organization and the job in question. Ask them to write down the names of three or four people who, in their view, are or were excellent employees in this job. There is no need for them to reveal the names of the people concerned, merely to think of a number of successful job holders. The test should be 'We would be very happy to employ this person again'. Then do the same for the poor employee. Get the group to think of three or four people who didn't come up to scratch, for whatever reason. They left, they failed, they upset people, they were poor communicators, they had their hand in the till, whatever it was. The test this time is 'We would not have employed these people if we had known then what we know now'.

Then draw up a list with two columns, one headed Successes, the other Failures. Under the Successes column, get the group to decide on characteristics which the successful hirings had in common. Then do the same with the Failures column.

PERSON SPECIFICATION: **Secretary**

ESSENTIAL CHARACTERISTICS

Physical
Articulate
Clear speech
Neat and tidy appearance

Attaintments
Shorthand: Minimum 100 wpm (Pitmans) or equivalent.
Typing: Minimum 50 wpm RSA Stage III or equivalent.
English Language at GCE 'O' level or CSE Grade 1, or RSA Stage III
Word processor (Wordstar) experience
2 years secretarial experience

Aptitudes
Good with words (oral and written)
Good telephone manner
Sound basic arithmetic

Interests
None in particular

Disposition
Acceptable to others
Self reliant
Sense of humour
Personable (enjoy and capable of mixing with a wide variety of people)
Dependable
Tact

Motivation
Successful candidate will be motivated by pleasant and friendly environment, being of service to others and working for a prestigious organization.

Circumstances
The job calls for a man or woman living within reasonable travelling distance of the workplace and willing to work occasional overtime

Salary scale
£5,500–£6,500 (rising by fixed annual increments)

Other benefits
Productivity bonus up to 10% per annum

Figure 2.4: Eight-point plan specification for a secretary

Prayer

Text

Appositeness

Action, voice, tone and style
(Presbyterian, Ordinary, Stiff and schoolboy-like)*

Age

Countenance
(Tolerable, Grave, Very Good)*

Length
(Convenient, Five Quarters, An hour)*

Within Book i.e. Well Read

Learning
(Little, Much Latin, None)*

Orthodoxness

* These are three-point scales.

Figure 2.5: Assessment for chaplaincy at Bridgewell (Source: Samuel Pepys, Secretary to the Navy, 1665)

Keep the words or phrases to describe each side of the chart very specific. Do not allow the group to resort to phrases like 'he was an effective negotiator' or 'she always treated clients in the right way'. The whole purpose is to use the list as a benchmark for candidates. Be very specific, otherwise you will never know how to assess whether a candidate is likely to perform in the same way or not. Figure 2.6 gives an example.

3. *Critical incidents*
This technique goes back a long way and is well known. Critical incidents are those key 'make or break' behaviours needed on the job and which distinguish the good performer from the also-ran. What you do is ask people who know about the target job (the

DESCRIPTIONS OF TEACHERS WHO WERE:

Successes	Failures
Prepared lessons well in advance	Rarely prepared lessons
Arrived in classroom on time	Arrived late and left early
Were friendly but firm with pupils	Intimidated by 'difficult' pupils
Assessed pupils' work regularly	Rarely set or marked work
Kept abreast of changes in the curriculum	Were out of date
Imaginative in presentation of lessons	Unimaginative in lesson presentation
Sensitive to different levels of pupil ability	Insensitive to the needs of less able pupils

Figure 2.6: Teachers' list

job you are trying to fill) to tell you about specific critical incidents which happen on the job.

Your questioning might go something like this.

Q. Tell me about an occasion at work where you did exactly the right thing, and had a real success.

A. Well, there was the time that I tried to sell to one of the big eight accountancy firms. I knew they were interested, but they were taking a long while to make up their minds. Every week I either phoned or wrote to them. Nothing pushy. I just reminded them of what we could offer, and that we would be interested in supplying. It took six months, but in the end they gave us our largest contract to date.

Continue to question and probe success like this. And ask other job holders. If these other examples support this first story, you can conclude that perseverance, or determined 'stickability', is one essential requirement for effective performance. It separates the good from the mediocre. It is one of the key elements in the person specification.

The other part of the technique is to ask about failures. You might ask:

Q. Now tell me about an occasion where you did exactly the wrong thing, and made a real mess of things.

A. Well, there was an occasion where I completely misjudged the person I was meeting. From her job title, I thought she would know all about our type of data processing system. So I went off into a spiel about the technical ins and outs. She didn't say anything. So I left after half an hour, leaving her with some technical material, thinking I'd done OK. Afterwards I heard that she thought I was a complete boffin and didn't want to see me again. She thought I couldn't communicate. In fact, I just didn't pick up the clues.

Again, don't asume that one swallow makes a summer. Keep asking questions like this both with this individual and with others in the same job. At the end of the day, if most are saying the same thing, you have a good idea of what skills are needed in the job. In this case, it looks like listening skills and an ability to pitch your language at the right level for the audience. So here is anothe key ingredient for the person specification.

Continue like this with other critical incidents to build up a list for the person specification. Now you know what to try to assess in candidates.

4. *Repertory grid*

This is an in-depth, interview-based method. It is a bit like the checklist procedure of numer 2, though more sophisticated. The method itself and the analysis of results need explanation and training beyond the scope of this book. It should preferably be carried out by a trained psychologist. It may be well worth the expense, though, in view of the costs of getting selection wrong.

Cautionary words about person specifications

1. When someone leaves a job, it is very easy to fall into the trap of writing the person specification to describe that person, minus

all the weaknesses. Avoid the temptation of trying to fill the post with the impossible – the excellent ex-employee with all her knowledge of the job and the organization, but without her flaws. Concentrate, instead, on asking what the candidate *must* have, or be able to learn, to do the job well.

2. Avoid the trap of making the person specification over-idealistic. Be realistic. Avoid the superstar-type person specification. Make the profile wide enough so that you can find people who can and will do the job, but won't be over-qualified.

3. Make the qualities measurable, as far as is possible. Avoid vague generalizations like 'highly qualified', 'considerable experience', or 'nice personality'.

Key points

1. When a vacancy arises, decide whether there are alternatives to recruiting someone, such as automation, subcontract, secondment, etc.

2. There are three steps to deciding what sort of person fits the job.

    - Analyse the job
    - Describe the job
    - Draw up a person specification

3. Job analysis involves collecting information on the tasks and responsibilities of a job. This gives the basis for a written job description.

4. Job descriptions should contain the job's title, purpose, position in the organization, and key tasks.

5. Person specifications can be drawn up using common frameworks, such as the seven- or eight-point plan, or by interviews which establish the qualities required to be successful in the job.

3 Attracting a Pool of Applicants

'Underneath this flabby exterior is an enormous lack of character.'

Oscar Levant

Now that you have a good idea of what the job involves and the sort of people you are looking for, it is time to set about trying to find them.

Recruitment

This stage is about recruitment, not selection. It is about making sure that you have the right number of suitably qualified applicants so as to be able to select one or more for the jobs on offer.

If you intend to use a recruitment agency to do the job for you, then you can ignore this chapter. But just before you turn the pages, it's worth remembering that it is an expensive business. Typical fees for recruitment consultants are 15% of the new employee's salary. Also, recruitment agencies are not always good at understanding what employers are looking for. Why not consider doing it yourself? If so, read on. Otherwise, see you in Chapter 4.

Recruitment is an important topic. Interviewing, testing and other methods of selecting can do nothing to improve the quality of the field of candidates. No amount of sophistication in picking the right people will compensate for a poor applicant pool from which to draw. All it will do is prove that none of them should be taken on. So how should we go about it? The first step is to decide how many to get into the frame.

How many recruits is enough?

Earlier I said that it is important to ensure the 'right number' of applicants from which to draw your chosen one or two. How do you know what this right number is?

Some people say that this number need be no more than the number of vacancies to be filled just so long as the candidates are the right people. But at the start of the selection process you don't yet know if they are the right people. Even if they turn out to be, it is a risky manoeuvre. They could refuse the offer, be run over by a bus the day before you take them on, or just have a change of heart.

To go to the other extreme, and have hundreds of applicants for each job, is just as foolish. If you do, there is the administrative headache of pre-selection – trying to reduce the applicant pool to manageable proportions.

The ideal is to have around six to eight candidates per vacancy, with most, if not all, of them suitably qualified for the job. That isn't easy. The solution to getting this number of appropriate applicants is to use the right source to help you, or to advertise the job properly.

Where to go for recruits

There are loads of possible places you can go to get a pool of applicants. Which method is best depends on the nature of the vacancy. Some of the more popular ones are:

Internal advertisements
Existing employees
Vacancy boards
Schools, colleges and universities
Newspaper advertisements
Radio and television advertisements
Employment and recruitment agencies
Executive search consultants (headhunters)

Internal adverts are where the job is advertised 'in house' through internal newsletters, notice boards or memos. Some organizations, notably the civil service, call it 'trawling'. The method has the advantage that it is quick and cheap, and the applicant's strengths and weaknesses are likely to be well known to at least somebody in the organization. It is also good for morale. The workforce sees that the organization cares enough for its employees to offer them the chance of first refusal.

The disadvantage is that no new blood can be brought into the organization by this method. It can lead to complacency and stagnation. Internal promotion is a common way of recruiting to senior positions, but this may be just the sort of post for which new ideas and approaches, and different experiences, may be most beneficial. The employer needs to weigh the morale advantage against the 'fresh mind to the problems' advantage.

Existing employees can often help you to find new recruits. They can pass on to friends and relations the news that you are looking to take on staff. It is a common method in manual jobs. The advantage is that the applicant can find out a lot about the job and the company from someone who knows. This helps to prevent the common frustration of new recruits that they have been 'sold a pup' when they discover the job doesn't live up to expectations. It is also cheap.

A potential problem is that you can unintentionally but indirectly discriminate against certain types of worker (see Chapter 12). This can happen if you rely on word of mouth recommendations to the exclusion of other sources of new recruits. Then only one ethnic or racial group may be selected, to the disadvantage of others who aren't on the grapevine.

Vacany boards are another very easy source of recruits. You often find them outside factories, advertising vacancies usually for skilled and semi-skilled workers. Again, it is cheap and quick, and relies on attracting people who work or live close to the site. The snag is that constant advertising for the same job can lead people to believe (perhaps correctly) that the conditions of work are poor and so people don't stay. So the company gets a bad reputation, deserved or undeserved.

Contact with educational institutions is becoming increasingly important for those who recruit young people, with the drop off in the supply of school leavers and certain graduates (see Chapter

1). A 1988 CBI report noted that both business and schools have a vital interest in forging effective local links between each other.

Many employers are stepping up their liaison with schools and colleges. At its most simple, you can write to a school or college. In my role as director of a post-graduate course at a university, I am often sent details of job offers to pass on to students. These get posted on notice boards or circulated around, and are seen by lots of people who might be interested. It is a very cost effective way for employers to bring the vacancy to a wide audience of prospective candidates.

You could establish more formal links. This might include you or other senior managers visiting schools, becoming a school governor, or helping teach courses (perhaps in management or your profession) at colleges, polytechnics and universities. One company, BP, has had links with schools for more than eight years and now spends £800,000 a year on school projects. You can bet that it does this for more reasons than just getting well-trained recruits, such as good community relations, PR and getting children familiar with its products. But it must help recruitment enormously.

Many employers do all the recruiting themselves. You may be one of these. If so, then you will usually have to advertise. *Newspapers* are where most adverts appear, though there is also *television and radio* to consider. If you decide to go down this route, you will have to make many decisions about the advertisement including which newspaper to place it in, for how long, what days of the week, how large the display should be, what should be said, and so on.

You will have noticed that some newspapers are better than others for certain types of advertisements. And certain days of the week are best for particular jobs. Always get copies of the newspapers you are interested in using, to see which and when is best. If in doubt, ring the advertisement section of the paper and ask which day is best for your vacancy.

Lots of research has been done on what attracts people to read adverts, and how they should be displayed. The results don't always coincide with common wisdom. A check list of good advice, based on this research, is shown in Figure 3.1.

1. Don't automatically choose the paper you happen to read. Consider what paper the *candidates* are likely to read.

2. The information the advertisement contains counts for more than the way it is presented.

3. The advert should start with a clear headline of what the job is. Ignore gimmicks.

4. Give as full a job description as you can in the space allowed.

5. Advertisements which do not state the salary are disliked. Unless there are very good reasons for not giving it, do so. Include benefits.

6. State what requirements are essential and what are desirable. Avoid restricting it to an age band without very good reason.

7. Watch out not to offend the Sex Discrimination or Race Relations Acts (see Chapter 12).

8. Don't worry about the position of the advert on the page. Research suggests that this is unimportant to readers. Size of advertisement is also relatively unimportant.

9. Composite adverts, where more than one job is advertised by the same recruiter, tend to be disliked by senior candidates, even if it does save the recruiter money.

10. Tell people clearly how to respond. Is an application form required or can they use a CV?

11. Avoid using box numbers. It puts people off from replying.

12. Very important: handle enquiries and reply to applications quickly. Never fail to reply. It gives a very bad impression of the company or the agency.

Figure 3.1: Guidelines for good newspaper job advertisements

Box 1 shows an unusual advert, placed in the year 1900. How well do you think it stacks up against the modern guidelines?

BOX 1

Men Wanted For Hazardous Journey

Small wages, bitter cold, long months of complete darkness, constant danger, safe return doubtful.
Honour and recognition in case of success.

(Advertisement for men to accompany an Antarctic expedition, placed by Sir Edward Shackleton in 1900. No relation to author!)

Employment agencies abound. They tend to specialize in certain occupations such as secretarial, nursing, accounting or computer staff. Typically they will charge you a fee of one month's salary or 15% of the salary for filling the vacancy. Many also supply temporary staff, again for certain occupations like secretarial, accounting or book-keeping, where an hourly, daily or weekly rate is charged. The advantages are that it passes the chore of finding people to an outside agency. But it still requires you to consider carefully the job description, the candidate requirements for the job (the person specification), and how you will assess them. Without this information the agency is unlikely to be able to select the appropriate person for you. Another disadvantage is cost, plus the fact that many agencies don't have enough people of the right calibre on their books.

Recruitment agencies again charge fees and tend to specialize in certain occupations such as technical, clerical or managerial. Recruitment agencies differ from employment agencies by their concentration on higher-level appointments. This means that often they have to put in greater effort to find people, which is reflected in higher fees. There are hundreds around, most of them concerned with management recruitment. In my experience, they vary a great deal in their level of expertise and professionalism. They do take away a lot of the drudgery of drawing up a list of suitable applicants, and are particularly useful if you don't have the time or expertise to do the job yourself. But you pay for the pleasure. Recruitment agencies don't come cheap, although they can be cost effective. Their fees depend on the level of service you require, as well as the level of the job, but figures of 15% or more of the successful candidate's remuneration package are not uncommon. They will draw up a shortlist of candidates, who are usually found by advertising. They will take responsibility for designing and placing the adverts, conducting initial interviews, sending the shortlisted candidates' curriculum vitae (CVs), and preparing a short report of their interview findings for you. A typical recruitment consultant's report on a candidate, illustrating what you might expect to receive, is shown in Figure 3.2.

Headhunters, or executive search consultants as they like to be called, are a special form of recruitment agency. Their main business is finding suitable candidates where the supply is limited. In effect, this means that their services tend to be confined to top jobs. You would probably not want to use them for levels lower than heads of divisions or departments.

Mostly they approach potential candidates directly, rather than through advertisements. This is supposedly because top people aren't actively looking for jobs or are too busy to scan job adverts. I say 'supposedly'. A recent survey by the executive selection division of accountants Price Waterhouse casts doubt on this assumption. Around 65% of executives, ranging from middle managers to directors, claimed to regularly read job advertisements, whether they were looking for jobs or not. More than 40% read appointments advertisements as often as twice a week.

Such a direct recruitment method as phoning round prospective candidates makes it a time consuming, discreet and delicate business. Consultants have to build trust and maintain confidentiality with prospective candidates. They have to check out their performance in their present and past jobs. On the client side, headhunters often have to help them negotiate remuneration packages with the people taken on.

How to choose an agency or consultant

So you've decided you could do with some help. How do you decide on which consultant or agency to use?

One of the best ways to decide which agency or consultant to

Henry Ambition

A slim, neat looking man of thirty-seven with a pronounced Newcastle accent and a very bright personality.

He went to secondary school in Newcastle where he was never interested in academic pursuits and left as soon as he could. He joined the Ministry of Defence as a craft apprentice where he qualified as an engineering technician. During this time he acquired an HNC in mechanical engineering.

After five years, he joined Garden Appliances Limited (GAL) in Warwick as a Design Engineer. He spent four years at GAL. The products were lawn mowers, barbecues, hedge trimmers and garden gnomes. He worked on most of the processes involved including presswork, injection moulding and assembly.

He managed to get himself sponsored by GAL on a full time MBA course at Warwick University. He found this a particularly useful year giving him a much greater appreciation of finance, sales and marketing and general management.

Having completed his MBA he . . .

. . . He has been with the present company six years, but recent events at Group level in the company have caused him some unease. He is therefore looking to move on.

He is currently Works Director covering two factory units, one in Glasgow and one in Carlisle. He has between 300 and 400 employees under his control (including part timers) and is a member of the Board. The Company has a turnover of approximately £30m and he reports to the Divisional Managing Director.

Comments

A very bright man who has a lot of manufacturing experience. I think he is capable of handling complex situations and dealing with many problems at the same time.

If he is sufficiently attracted by the position (and he claims to be so following my talk with him) then I think he would give you tremendous value for money. He is looking at his career at present and could be tempted for the right package. He is obviously ambitious and feels that there are no further opportunities in his present job.

Figure 3.2: Typical Recruitment Consultant's Report on a Candidate

choose is on recommendation. Ask other employers or other business contacts who they use. Probe their experience of agencies for your industry or target job.

Alternatively, contact a professional organization. The names and addresses of the Institute of Personnel Management, the British Institute of Management and the British Psychological Society are given in the Appendix of this book. So are the names and addresses of some of the bigger selection consultancies.

Don't just choose those who pester you with phone calls.

Checklist of questions you should ask consultants

Once you have got two or three possible consultants in mind, you'll want to try to discover if they will do a good job for you. This isn't easy from an initial meeting, as I will be saying about selection interviews. Some things you will want to know are:

1. How much experience do you have of selection or recruitment consultancy?
2. How long have you done this sort of work?
3. What did you do before consultancy?
4. What other organizations have you done similar work for?
5. Can you give me permission to contact some of these people?
6. What are your fees and terms of business?
   Get these in writing
7. Who exactly will be handling my assignment?
   Don't be fooled into believing that the person you meet first will necessarily work on the assignment. Ask to meet the people you will be directly working with.

Why should a candidate come to work for you?

While you are concentrating on getting a pool of applicants together, think also what you can offer candidates. Selection is a two-way street. The main aim of this book is to help you choose between applicants, but candidates are choosing as well. School leavers and graduates may be choosing between different types of jobs, between bank clerk or secretary, for example. People of whatever age choose between organizations offering jobs, between Marks and Spencer, Woolworth and Sainsbury, for example. They choose whether to apply to you and then whether to accept, if offered the job. The exceptions are few. Some people are very unfussy (so do you really want them?). Some have very limited choice because they have few skills, or live in an area of very high unemployment. The majority have choice. And more and more we are seeing a shift to a seller's market, with demographic changes in the number of young people (see Chapter 1).

It is very important that you communicate what the job is all about to the candidate or prospective candidate. You owe it to applicants and to yourself to give them a realistic overview of what the job involves. You will save yourself and the successful applicant a lot of grief if you do.

What seems to happen is that people both self-assess and assess the job. In other words, they compare themselves with what the job involves. They may say to themselves: 'From what I know of this job in this company and thinking of what I'm like, this job would suit me nicely. So I'll apply.' Or they may say to themselves: 'I'm restless, ambitious and money-mad. I love a challenge. That's just the way I am. This employer seems stodgy, complacent, stingy with money, and going nowhere fast. I'll not bother to send in this application form.'

The same sort of process takes place when deciding whether to accept an offer, only now they usually have more information. It's your job to see that they have the necessary information at each stage.

Telling it like it is: realistic job previews

There are lots of ways you can communicate to applicants what the job is all about. You can send them brochures, pamphlets, company magazines, or books about the company and the jobs on offer. We'll be looking at brochures in detail in a minute. Bcfore that stage, you could make visits to schools or colleges to talk about the organization and the jobs it offers. For more experienced people, show them round the buildings, the factory, store, office, or whatever. Let them talk to people. Let them get the feel of the place. With graduates, many employers invite candidates up the night before the assessment day to meet and have an evening meal with last year's intake. This is an excellent idea.

Recent methods of communication are videos, which are useful if there are a lot of applicants. Invite them to come and watch the video before the site visit. Or arrange for it to be shown at careers offices at universities and polytechnics.

There is no substitute for the first-hand experience of actually doing the job. Think about the probationary periods, although admittedly these are expensive for organization and the individual concerned. Or get students in for holiday jobs. With undergraduates, think about offering places to students on sandwich courses, who have work experience varying from a few weeks to a whole year as part of their studies. Then both of you have the opportunity for a good long look at one another.

Another way of giving a feel of part of the job is work samples. This tests candidates on a small part of the job. It shows you how well he is likely to do, and shows the applicant what the job is like. Chapter 10 looks at this in more detail.

All these ways of communicating the job have been called *realistic job previews*. They are not just a chance for you to glamorize the job or do a snow job on applicants. It is an opportunity to convey the image and the feel of the organization, genuine but hopefully attractive. Above all, the aim is to be *realistic* about the job to applicants. One study in an American telephone company showed what being a telephone operator was really like, warts and all. It showed that the job was routine, closely supervised, very fast-paced, and solitary. The only relief to the tedium was the occasional unpleasant or hostile customer! Yet the realism in the overview of the job allowed the company to increase its chances of getting people who would stick the job and even enjoy it.

Brochures

One major way in which organizations attempt to attract people, particularly students, to apply to them is through recruitment literature. This is typically a glossy brochure. These are left lying around careers offices in universities and colleges, or are sent to students who apply. Research suggests that brochures are very influential in shaping the perceptions graduates have of an organization. Since students have usually never worked before, except for part-time holiday jobs, they therefore know very little about what different companies are like to work for. Realistic previews become even more important. That is where the glossy brochure comes in.

What makes a good brochure?

What makes a brochure that will stimulate a student to fill in the application form stuffed in the back? Research by myself and a colleague at Aston Business School has thrown light on this question.

Students judge a brochure in three ways. They are:

STYLISHNESS
INFORMATION
FRIENDLINESS

Stylishness is a very important factor. Students like brochures to be appealing, trendy, slick, glossy, attractive to hold and look at. A stylish brochure gets high marks from students. But this is not enough on its own.

The second factor is information. Students look for useful, relevant, clearly presented facts about the company and the job. Pay, conditions of work, types of training offered, the 'feel' of the organization in which they will work, the nature of the job itself, are some of the more important pieces of information they look for.

Finally, students are concerned with *how* this information is got across. They like the brochure to be friendly. They like it to talk to them in a personal way. They like to feel they are being addressed as individuals. Not an easy thing to get across when the brochure is aimed at thousands of different individuals, but it is what students want, and what brochure designers need to grapple with. One way is to have 'pen portraits' of recent student appointments telling the reader about the job. Another is 'a day in the life of' a new recruit. That way the reader has a chance to identify with the job. Do bear in mind, though, that what is good design for one company is not necessarily the same as another's. They have to be tailor-made.

There are numerous agencies which specialize in recruitment advertising literature, like brochures. Some are listed in the Appendix. Professional companies will be familiar with methods of getting student impressions of brochures. But as in all things, if you decide to do it yourself, think carefully about what the readers need to know and how they like to have it presented. Try out the literature with students. There's no better way of getting an opinion, sometimes not very flattering, but invaluable!

Key points

1. Recruitment is about obtaining a sufficiently large pool of suitable applicants from which to select.

2. You have a wide choice of recruitment sources. You can use:

    - Internal advertisements
    - Existing employees
    - Vacancy boards
    - Schools, colleges and universities
    - Newspaper advertisements
    - Radio and television advertisements
    - Employment agencies
    - Recruitment agencies
    - Executive search consultants (headhunters)

3. Candidates are also in the selection business. They need an opportunity to learn what is involved in the job, both its tastes and distastes. This helps avoid future disappointments for both you and them.

4. You can do this by offering applicants a realistic preview of the job. This includes:

    - Talks
    - Videos
    - Brochures
    - Visits to the site
    - Samples of the work to be done
    - Probationary periods
    - Vacation work for students

4 Selection Exercise

'I hear and I forget
I see and I remember
I do and I understand' *Chinese Proverb*

Company Selection

In this exercise, you will find notes on three candidates (two of them external and one internal) who have been shortlisted for the position of Branch Manager in the We-haul Distribution Co. Ltd.

Instructions

You are asked to:

1. Carry out an analysis on each of the candidates and compare the results with the person specification.
2. Place the candidates in order of suitability for the position.
3. If your favoured candidate decided not to accept the offer, would you appoint your second choice or would you re-advertise?
4. What other information, if any, would you require about the candidates to carry out a realistic assessment?

Have a go at it. You will find a spare sheet to write on after the job and candidate details. Then turn to my suggested method and answer.

WE-HAUL DISTRIBUTION CO. LTD

JOB DESCRIPTION

JOB TITLE Branch Manager (Birmingham)

1. **Main purpose of the job**

   To plan, organize and control the resources and activities of the branch so as to provide the required levels of service to our customers and to, at least, meet budgeted revenue, productivity and expenditure targets.
   To expand branch activities in existing and developing products profitably.

2. **Position in the organization**

   (a) Directly responsible to General Manager, Midlands and North.

   (b) Functional links with We-haul Branch Management Team.

   (c) Directly manages:
   Assistant Branch Manager
   Operations Controller
   Senior Traffic Clerk

3. **Scope of the job**

   Responsibility for staff numbers, fleet and property, resources as budgeted and altered with operational requirements.

4. **Limits of authority**

   (a) **Expenditure:** May spend up to £100 for any one contingency.

   (b) **Operations:** Required to optimize branch operational plan, constantly updating and improving collection and delivery rounds.

   (c) **Staff:** Recruit within budgeted establishment, unless othewise directed. Undertake disciplinary enquiries and award punishments within the Disciplinary Policy and Procedure.

5. **Key tasks**

(a) **Staff management:** To manage total workforce employed at the branch through supervisory team so as to enable each individual to achieve his or her performance target. To hold regular meetings with all persons employed as Supervisors and Foremen, in order to maintain effective communications within the branch.

(b) **Budgets and Management Control:** To prepare the Branch budget and forward plans in connection with advice from We-haul Group General Manager and to monitor and control actual performance.

(c) **Operations:** To cost-effectively operate, where appropriate, trunk, handling, collection and delivery, warehousing and other services within the overall framework of satisfying the needs of his or her own customers and the Company's service objectives.

(d) **Administration:** To administer, safeguard and control the cash and other assets at the branch, safeguard customers' goods, in accordance with Company procedures, so as to satisfy all audit requirements and customers' enquiries and claims.

(e) **Marketing:** To maintain existing originated traffic levels and seek new and profitable business, so as at least to meet budgeted revenue value and expenditure targets.

(f) **Legislations:** To ensure that the provision of the Health and Safety at Work Act, Construction and Use Regulations, Traffic Acts, etc. are observed within the branch and on the highway.

(g) **Communications:** To ensure that all key staff are kept well informed on matters which vitally concern and affect them. This provision applies equally to information flowing up to the General Manager and his/her staff, as to the provision and interpretation of information to her/his own subordinates.

(h) **Business Development:** To seek out and exploit new opportunities for profitable development of the branch, including diversification into areas of potential growth, e.g. engineering services, express services, contract hire, etc.

Standards by which performance will be measured will include:

a) Performance against budget and previous experience (in order to ensure continuous achievement of improving results) on revenue, volumes, productivity and expenditure levels.

b) Company service objectives as regularly refined and updated regarding 24 Hour Express, Network and Mail Order traffic.

c) Maintain an effective after sales service to ensure existing revenue is fully protected, enquiries are dealt with within the specified time scale and non-traced enquiries are thoroughly investigated prior to payment of claims.

d) Develop an effective Management and Supervisory team with a highly results-orientated framework.

e) Maintain good industrial relations through effective use of the consultative machinery for maximum harmony and efficiency in the work force.

PERSON SPECIFICATION

(An interpretation of the job description in terms of the kind of person suitable for the job.)

1. **Physical characteristics**

   ESSENTIAL:
   Good health record.
   No significant disabilities in voice, hearing and eyesight.
   Tidy, conventional dress.

   DESIRABLE:
   Well turned out and takes trouble with details of personal appearance.

2. **Attainments**

   ESSENTIAL:
   Either Education and/or professional qualifications not lower than degree standard; evidence of occupational success in previous employment; distribution management experience – minimum of five years after three to four years other business experience (not specific). Minimum age 30 years.

   Or at least five years supervisory and management experience in the freight transport industry. Minimum age 30 years.

   Plus in either case an understanding of scheduling work, programming, quality control and current legislation and experience of negotiating with trade unions at plant level.

   DESIRABLE:
   A recognized qualification in business management.

3. **Intelligence**

   ESSENTIAL:
   Top 20%
   Demonstrates an intelligent approach to business problem solving

4. **Aptitudes**

ESSENTIAL:
Oral and written fluency.
Analytical skills.
Ability to prepare and understand basic statistical information.
Arithmetical competence.
Ability to read balance sheets and profit and loss accounts, and understand their significance.
High degree of listening skill.
Evidence of ability to plan ahead and organize the work of others within a general policy framework.
Skills of conciliation.

5. **Interests**

ESSENTIAL:
Nothing specific.

6. **Disposition**

ESSENTIAL:
Acceptability to other people and previous occupational evidence of influencing others. Able to accept responsibility without undue strain. Generally constructive in relationships with others.

CONTRA-INDICATION:
Aggressive and impatient.

7. **Motivation**

ESSENTIAL:
Ambitious – evidence of fairly rapid promotion and the achievement of high but realistic goals.

8. **Circumstances**

ESSENTIAL:
Ability to work long and unusual hours if required and willingness to work at weekends when necessary.

1. EXTERNAL CANDIDATE

Bryn Brian Morgan – Traffic Office Supervisor (Round-Britain Freight Consortium)

Bryn Morgan is 33 years old, Welsh, and an only child. His father was a miner in Wales and his mother a Welsh-language teacher. He was educated at the local Swansea primary and secondary schools up to the age of 16 and he left with six GCE O-level passes including Mathematics and English.

He became a clerk in a house insulation firm for 18 months and then joined See-Through Double Glazing as a Salesman. After a further two years he joined the East Midland Gas Board as a trainee and after three months was appointed to the position of Work Study Officer. After three and a half years he joined his present company as a Work Study Officer, but within six months became an assistant to the Platform Controller at a major distribution depot. After three years he became Platform Controller and 18 months ago, Traffic Officer Supervisor.

In his job as Platform Controller he was involved in procedural (grievances and discipline) negotiations with shop stewards. His role as Traffic Officer Supervisor is to control the Traffic Office ensuring completion of all duties, fully using staff available and maintaining relations with customers.

He is married with two children, 6 and 2 years. He spends most of his spare time with his family who are very important to him. Most of his interests are centred around the home. He enjoys gardening, D-I-Y, making home-made wine and beer and listening to classical music. He sings in a local male-voice choir.

Bryn Morgan is quite ambitious and sees it as his duty to his family to seek promotion. But he is not willing to achieve success at the expense of his family.

He tends to take himself very seriously and regards attention to detail as being very important. He has very high standards himself and expects others to have the same. This leads him at times to be rather intolerant of the shortcomings of others and he can come over to his subordinates as being rather authoritarian.

However, he has the reputation of getting good results. His colleagues are divided in their opinion of him. There are those who think very highly of him and others who dislike his lack of humour and rather bossy manner.

He is somewhat defensive about the fact that he does not have formal qualifications, but regards practical experience as much more important. He sees himself very much as a 'professional manager'.

2. EXTERNAL CANDIDATE

Anne Swithin – Assistant Branch Manager, Mega Transport Co.

Anne Swithin is 35 years old, married with no children. She was born, one of five children, into a working class family on the outskirts of Oldham. She attended Shireburn School until the age of fifteen. A year earlier her father had died, and although she was thought by her teachers to be quite bright, for financial reasons she had to leave school and get a job.

She became a clerk in a small firm of accountants but continued her studies for GCE O-level at Manchester Technical College and subsequently obtained 3 A-level passes and a place at Exeter University to read History. She worked very hard and obtained an upper second class honours degree.

She joined Unilever as a Management Trainee, spending five years with them and finishing as a Production Manager. She then joined her present employer as an Assistant Branch Manager. Four years ago she obtained the Diploma in Management Studies (DMS) through day-release studies at a technical college. At present she is studying for a Master of Business Administration (MBA) degree part-time.

As Assistant Branch Manager, she has negotiated with shop stewards on grievances and pay. Her DMS course included work study, quality control and scheduling. In her present job she has been jointly responsible, with another person, for transport route planning and rostering.

Anne Swithin is very ambitious and has no outside interests, preferring to devote most of her energies to her job. She says that her husband takes second place and that he, too, is very much involved with his job. They try to keep at least Saturdays and Sundays free of work responsibilities, but she admits that this doesn't always happen.

She works extremely hard and for many hours. Although she could be described as meticulous rather than creative, she has come up with some innovative ideas on one or two occasions.

She has a reputation with subordinates for being a tough but fair boss and is respected for this. However, she does not suffer fools gladly and can be impatient with others if she feels that they are not doing their job properly. This has led to confrontations in the past.

3. INTERNAL CANDIDATE

Stuart Waterman – Operations Supervisor, Croydon

Stuart Waterman is 30 years old. He was born in Plymouth and brought up as an only child in a middle class home. He attended a local independent day school until the age of eleven, when, after passing the eleven plus, he went to St Joseph's School.

His school career was a successful one. As well as distinguishing himself in the GCE O-level and A-level examinations, he played for the first eleven at cricket and was a house captain and head boy in his last year. He went to Churchill College, Cambridge and obtained a second class honours in Physics. He continued to do well at sport and obtained a rowing blue and played for the College first eleven at cricket. A report from his tutor at the time said he was capable of getting a first class honours, but was rather lazy and spent too much time on sport.

He joined the company as a graduate trainee and after two years' experience in sales became Operations Foreman and three years ago Operations Supervisor. As Operations Supervisor he has negotiated with shop stewards on grievances and has sat in on plant pay negotiations as part of his development. His present job is to organize and control drivers and platform staff to achieve specified productivity and service levels.

He is unmarried and leads a full social life. He plays soccer and spends his summer weekends sailing. He has been to Switzerland for 2 weeks skiing every year for the last 10 years and counts these 2 weeks as sacred. Nothing gets in the way of this fortnight abroad. He has a wide circle of friends and enjoys going to the theatre and concerts, and dining out. He has already had some exotic foreign holidays and plans to do more.

Stuart Waterman is a person for whom success has come easily. He is ambitious, but sees promotion as a means of achieving a higher standard of living rather than for status or job satisfaction. His social life is very important to him.

He has an easy-going manner and a sense of humour. He generally gets on well with his colleagues, but he can be impatient with those he considers to be 'wimps' or bores. He is very creative and innovative, but occasionally gets carried away with his own enthusiasm. His more conservative colleagues think that he sometimes takes unnecessary risks, and some are jealous of the apparent ease with which he achieves success.

A. **Notes on appearance and some aspects of behaviour during the selection procedure**

BRYN MORGAN

CLOTHES: Light brown suit; slightly creased; cream shirt; brown tie; brown shoes.
HAIR: Brown; straight; short.
HEIGHT: 5′10″. Weight: 12 stone 7lbs.

Non-smoker.
Welsh accent; tense and on the defensive at times; rather ponderous in manner but articulate.

ANNE SWITHIN

CLOTHES: Navy suit; classically smart; white blouse; navy shoes.
HAIR: Brown; curly; medium length.
HEIGHT: 5′5″. Weight: 9 stone 12lbs.

Smoker.
Rather tense at first but became more relaxed. Speaks rather slowly taking time to weigh up her words. Slight Lancashire accent.

STUART WATERMAN

CLOTHES : Dark blue suit, smart and well-pressed; light blue shirt; college tie; grey suede shoes.
HAIR: ginger, balding.
HEIGHT: 5′9″. Weight: 11 stone 3lbs.

Non-smoker.
Very relaxed; no regional accent; speaks quickly but clearly; articulate and confident.

B. **Notes on intelligence, physical features and circumstances**

All candidates have taken a battery of numerical and verbal reasoning (intelligence) tests and are within the range stipulated in the Person Specification. They all have a satisfactory health record and have passed the medical examination.

Each candidate claims that there are no family circumstances which would prevent him/her working long and unusual hours and weekends if required.

C. **Notes on contributions to a group discussion held during the selection procedure**

Note: there were originally 6 people in the group discussion, but the shortlist now contains only the 3 here.

Bryn Morgan
Quiet. Only spoke infrequently. When he did, his points were generally listened to by the rest of the group and often taken up. Provided some new ideas, a number of which were challenged by Waterman.

Anne Swithin
Opened the discussion and played the chairperson's role throughout. When the discussion flagged she put in new ideas and tried to bring everyone in at all times. She gained little support for her views from the rest of the group. She extended existing discussion points to bring out new topics.

Stuart Waterman
Spoke frequently. Provided lots of new ideas. Rather critical of the ideas of others. Analysed problems very well. Injected humour into the proceedings. Didn't listen much to other people.

OTHER DATA

1. Retirement age in the company is 60.

2. The location of the Branch is at Birmingham.

3. The salary scale for the Branch Manager's position is: £18,000–£22,000.

4. Current salaries:

Morgan	£15,000
Swithin	£17,100
Waterman	£16,160

5. Organization structures at the large plants (e.g. Birmingham, Glasgow, Bromley, Southampton)

Branch Manager
|
Assistant Branch Manager
|
Senior Platform Supervisor
(Operations Supervisor)
| |
Platform supervisor Platform supervisor

YOUR METHOD AND ANSWER

Notes on your method

Candidates in order of suitability

What other information would you need for a realistic assessment?

My method and answer

The first thing to note is that there is no 'right' answer. Although based in reality, this is an exercise to get you thinking. But my suggested methods apply to real selection as well as to this exercise.

How to approach the problem

1. *Refer to the person specification*
Whichever method you use, you should concentrate on deciding who best meets the requirements of the job. These are laid out in the person spec. Carefully compare each candidate with each requirement.

2. *Look for evidence in the past*
A rule of thumb is: 'The best predictor of future success is past success.' Look to see which candidate has best succeeded in circumstances similar to the job on offer. Look for evidence that the applicant is able and willing to do the job.

3. *Look to see if all the evidence is there*
If you have doubts about the candidate's past, ask at interview. Ask for evidence that the candidate has coped well with work responsibilities. Look for gaps in what is required and what the candidate seems capable of doing. Look for holes in the CV. Did you notice that Bryn Morgan has a gap of around three or four years in his career history? It may be just a slip when he wrote out his application form. It may be something else. Either way it's missing data. Ask about it.

If you need more evidence, think about testing or work sampling.

Method

Here is a method which works best for me when I'm selecting people. It is based on numbers as well as feelings and compares candidates on each job requirement step by step.

1. *The importance of each attribute*
The first step is to examine the person specification. Look at each of the eight points in turn and decide how important each is to the successful accomplishment of the job. Ignore the candidates at this stage.

Take physical characteristics and its definition first. Ask yourself how important this is to success in the job, bearing in mind the job description. Give it a score between 1 and 10 to represent its importance relative to the other seven attributes. Then turn to the next one, attainments, and do exactly the same. And so on.

You will see my attempt below. I think that physical characteristics, as defined in the person spec, are relatively unimportant. It doesn't matter too much how smartly turned out the applicant is, within reason. Similarly, health problems only matter if they are extreme. So I have given it a weighting score of 2. On the other hand, I feel that attainments are very important here. Education and relevant experience are vital to be able to do the job well. I've given it a weight of 10. Intelligence is less important than attainments, but more important than appearance, so I've awarded it a 6.

Attributes	*Weight*
Physical characteristics	2
Attainments	10
Intelligence	6
Aptitudes	10
Interests	3
Disposition	8
Motivation	7
Circumstances	7

2. *Scoring each candidate*
Now comes the turn of the candidates. From the candidate blurb, decide how well each of them meets the attributes in the eight-point plan. Give a score to each candidate for all eight points. Ignore for now the attribute weighting of the previous section.

Let's take the example of physical characteristics. Both Anne and Stuart were smartly turned out and there is no evidence of health problems. I might want to ask my preferred candidate to take a medical exam at a later stage, but for now they are in the clear. So I've given each of them a 10. Bryn has a crumpled suit, though not badly so, so I gave him a 7. Remember that I am ignoring my view that appearance is only minimally relevant for success.

With attainments, I gave Anne a score of 10. She has all the education and experience I am looking for. Bryn again scores a bit lower. He doesn't have any educational or professional qualifications, and his time in the road freight industry is only just enough. I gave him a 5. Stuart falls somewhere between the other two, so I gave him 8.

I now have a table that look like this:

Attributes	*Weight*		*Bryn*	*Anne*	*Stuart*
Physical characteristics	2	×	7	10	10
Attainments	10	×	5	10	8
Intelligence	6	×	9	9	9
Aptitudes	10	×	7	9	5
Interests	3	×	7	1	5
Disposition	8	×	5	6	7
Motivation	7	×	4	10	6
Circumstances	7	×	4	10	5
			305	455	352

You will see that I have put a multiplication sign by the attribute weights. I have multiplied the weight in the left-hand column with each score given a candidate in the three right-hand columns. Totalling up these new, weighted candidate scores gives me the figures at the bottom of the columns.

The decision

Candidates in order of suitability:

1. Anne Swithin
2. Stuart Waterman
3. Bryn Morgan

My conclusion is that Anne is the best candidate, Stuart comes second and Bryn third. If everything else looks OK, I'll offer Anne the job. If she turns me down, I'll approach Stuart.

Advantages and disadvantages of the method

Advantages

Comparing candidates is difficult whatever method you use. I prefer a numerical system like this. For me, it is:

- Logical and systematic.
- Fair. It reduces the chance that biases and prejudices will creep in unnoticed.
- Especially useful if the selection is being done by more than one person. It helps us compare our results. It focuses attention on differences we have either about the importance of the job criteria or the worth of different candidates.

Disadvantages

- Numbers are often seductive. People sometimes assume that if there is a number attached it *must* be right. Of course, that doesn't follow at all. But numbers may lead you into a false sense of security. In the end, it is a subjective judgement. Numbers don't get you away from that.

In summary

I recommend the method. One of the most difficult things in selection is to try to keep in mind all the time the question: 'What sort of person will make a good job of this post?' Getting it down on paper in a fair, clear and orderly way, helped by numbers, focuses the mind.

5 Application Forms

'The closest to perfection a person ever comes is when he fills out a job application form.'

Stanley J. Randall

What use are application forms?

A well-designed application form can be very useful to you in the business of selecting. It has lots of purposes. They are:

1. To help you screen. This is where you weed out the no-hopers and get down to a shortlist. Only well-constructed forms allow you to do this properly.

2. To give you pointers to look for and follow up in the interview.

3. To spot where the best candidates are coming from. Good application forms have a section asking how the candidate found out about the vacancy. This tells you where good applicants are coming from and so helps you decide what sources to use in the future. You may find that only certain trade journals, or only newspaper advertisements on certain days of the week, turn up a healthy supply of good applicants.

4. As good public relations exercise and company image builder. Lots of people will see your application form (you hope), even if only a few decide to apply. It portrays an image of your professionalism and efficiency. For the same reason it is important that you reply promptly, even to those you aren't intending to interview.

5. As information for the personnel file of the successful applicant. It will give you basic details like address, sex, age, job title, etc, which you will need to arrange pay, tax deductions, and so on.

Application form or CV?

For senior positions most people will have a CV to hand. So why bother to send them an application form?

The reasons stem, in part, from the purposes we looked at above. These are the market research which can be done so cheaply on the sources of candidates, and the company image that can be got across in a good application form. But there is more to it than that. The CV may well miss out information that you need, such as career aims, gaps in work history, driving record, or reason for leaving present employer. Also, comparing candidates in the initial sift, especially if there are a lot of them, is very difficult if you don't have the information laid out in a standard way.

Of course, there is nothing to stop you asking for a CV and, if it contains interesting material, using it as a prompt for interview questions. But I advise you to ask candidates to fill out an application form as well.

How many different application forms do I need?

At a pinch you could get away with one standard application form for all jobs, if it is broad enough in its questions, though this is far from ideal. At the other extreme, in a perfect world, you would have as many different application forms as there are jobs. The reason for this is that you need different information for different jobs. More practically, the minimum number for most organizations is three. You need one for those starting work (school and college leavers), one for professionals and managers, and one for other employees. The three basic forms I recommend you use are given in Figures 5.1, 5.2 and 5.3. They are taken from Smith and Robertson's book (see Appendix), with their permission and the permission of the publishers. You can copy them if you wish, but please acknowledge the original source.

School Leaver

APPLICATION FORM

Please return this form to:

No later than:

1. POSITION APPLIED FOR:

2. PERSONAL DETAILS:

Surname: ______________ Forenames: ______________

Address: ______________ Telephone No: ______________

______________ Date of Birth: ________ Age ___ yrs

______________ Place of Birth: ______________

____

Name and address of next of kin:

____

____

____

____

____

Occupation of next of kin ______________

Names of any friends or relatives already working with this company

____

____

____

3. SCHOOL HISTORY
(since age 11)

Names of schools attended	Dates	
______________	________ to	________
______________	________ to	________
______________	________ to	________

What school subjects did you *like* most

____

____

What school subjects did you *dislike* most

____

____

Please list all the examinations you have taken (if you are taking exams in the next few months, list them here but leave the results column blank)

subject	exam (e.g. CSE)	result

May we approach the headmaster of your last school for a reference? YES/NO

____

____

4. HOBBIES AND PASTIMES

What are your hobbies & pastimes?

Have you ever won any awards or prizes for your pastime?

Please give details of any spare-time job you have had:

from to
from to
from to

____

____

5. FUTURE PLANS

What sort of work interests you most?

What job would you like to be doing in 5 years' time?

---

6. GENERAL

When could you start work with this company?

How did you hear of us? (Give name of newspaper etc.)

Signed ______________________ Date ____________

THANK YOU FOR YOUR INTEREST IN THIS COMPANY

Figure 5.1: School leaver application form

APPLICATION FORM

Please return this form to:

No later than:

1. POSITION APPLIED FOR:

2. PERSONAL DETAILS:

   Surname:
   Forenames:
   Address:
   Telephone Number:
   Date of Birth:
   Marital Status:
   Ages of children (if any):

Name and address of next of kin:

Do any of your friends or relatives work for this company (give name)?

3. WORK HISTORY

   Name & address of your present (or last) employer:

   Title of job:
   Details of duties and type of work:

   Current salary:
   Date and job title when you started work with this employer:

   If you have already left your last job, give date of leaving:

Reason for leaving or wanting to change employers:

Name and address of your *last-but-one* employer:

Title of Job:

Details of duties and type of work:

Date and Job Title when you started work with this employer

Date of leaving and reason for leaving this employer

Names and addresses of other previous employers	Job Title	Dates	Reasons for Leaving

---

4. EDUCATION & TRAINING
(from age 11)

Please list the names and types of school and colleges you have attended — dates

Please list all the exams you have taken — results

Please list any training you have received. Include night school, day release, apprenticeship, in-company courses and correspondence courses

dates

---

5. MEDICAL HISTORY

Please list any serious illness you have had in the last 5 years. If you are a registered disabled person, give your certificate number.

Would you be willing to have a medical examination? Yes/No
Name and address of doctor

---

6. GENERAL

Please list any hobbies or pastimes you have and give details of any prizes or awards you have won. Also list any spare-time jobs.

When could you start work for this company?

How did you hear of us? (give name of newspaper etc.)

---

7. REFERENCES

Please give the names and addresses of THREE people who know your work. One should be your present (last) company – we will not approach your present employer without your permission. Do not give the names of relatives.

Signed Date

Figure 5.2: Senior management application form

APPLICATION FORM

Please return this form to:

Not later than:

1. POSITION APPLIED FOR

2. PERSONAL DETAILS

Surname: ________________ Forenames: ________________

Address: ________________ Telephone No: ________________

________________ Date of Birth: ________________

________________ Marital Status: ________________

________________ Ages of children (if any):

________________ __ yrs __ yrs __ yrs

__ yrs __ yrs __ yrs

Name and Address of next of kin:

____

________________________________ Telephone: __________

Names of friends or relatives in this company Position

________________________________ __________

________________________________ __________

________________________________ __________

3. WORK HISTORY

Name and address of your present (or last) employer:

____

____

Date and job title on starting: ______________________

Title of present job: ______________________

Brief indication of type of work:

____

Reason for leaving:

____

____

Salary of present (or last) job ______________________

If you have already left your last job, give the date of leaving:

____

Names and addresses of other previous employers	Job Title	Dates	Reasons for Leaving

4. EDUCATION AND TRAINING
(from age 11)

Names and type of school and colleges you have attended	dates

Please list all the examinations you have taken results

Please list any training you have received. Include night school, day release, apprenticeship, in-company courses and correspondence courses.

duration

__________________________________ _____ to _____

__________________________________ _____ to _____

---

5. <u>MEDICAL HISTORY</u>

Have you ever suffered from:

– Back trouble	Yes/No	When?
– Nervous troubles	Yes/No	When?
– Dermatitis	Yes/No	When?
– Alcoholism	Yes/No	When?
– Epilepsy	Yes/No	When?

Would you be willing to have a medical examination? Yes/No
Name and address of doctor

If you are a registered disabled person, give your certificate No.

---

6. <u>GENERAL</u>

What are your hobbies and pastimes?

Have you ever won any prizes or awards for your hobbies?

Please give details of any spare-time jobs you have had:

When could you start work with this company?

How did you hear of us? (give name of newspaper etc.)

---

7. REFERENCES

Please give the names and addresses of TWO people who know your work. One should be your present (last) company, but we will not approach your present employer without your permission. Do not give the names of any relatives.

______________________ ______________________

______________________ ______________________

______________________ ______________________

______________________ ______________________

______________________ ______________________

Please feel free to add any extra relevant information on a separate sheet

I certify that the information I have provided is correct

Signed ______________________ Date ______________

THANK YOU FOR YOUR INTEREST IN THIS COMPANY

Figure 5.3: Standard application form

Overleaf I have also included two examples of a good, 'real' application form from one of my clients, Helix Ltd, who kindly gave permission for them to be reproduced here. The first is broad enough to be used for a range of jobs from first job to executive, though is not really suitable for manual workers. They use the second one for factory workers.

PRIVATE AND CONFIDENTIAL –
APPLICATION AND PERSONAL RECORD

Position applied for ....

From what source did you ascertain this position was available ....

Surname .... Christian Names ....

Address ....

....

.... Tel. No ....

Age .... Date of Birth .... Nationality ....

Marital Status .... Number of Dependents .... Adults

Religion .... Children and Age(s)

Are you prepared to relocate ..... If yes when? ....

How much time are you prepared to spend away from home ....

....

Are you, or have you been, in business on your own account, if so, give details ....

....

Have you an interest in any other business ....

Do you possess a current Group 'A' Driving Licence ....

How long have you held a Driving Licence ....

Have you any Endorsements. Yes/No. If so, how many ....

Do you have the **complete** use of a Company car at present ....
(If so which Model)

What other benefits do you currently receive ....

Do you suffer any disability..

Have you ever suffered from any serious illness, if so state the nature of illness and date of occurrence ....

What is your height .... Weight ....

Please attach a recent photograph if available

EDUCATION

Dates From To	School or University	Courses Examinations Qualifications	Other Activities

WORKING LIFE (Current or Last employment at top)

Dates From To	Employer, Service Unit or other Organisation. Nature of Business	Location	Position or Rank	Respon-sible to

Professional Body and Date Elected	Referees (2 Previous immediate superiors + 1 personal ref.) N.B. References will only be contacted with your agreement.
	1.
	2.
	3.

Responsible for (including number of staff etc.)	Salary (inc. Bonus) Start Finish (or current)	Reason for Leaving or wishing to Leave:-

Languages			
Oral Fluency			
Written Fluency			

What do you feel qualifies you for this position ....
....
....
....
....

Please write short notes to cover the following:

(1) Short term business plans ....
....
....

(2) Long term business career plans ....
....
....

What job functions do you do particularly well ....
....
....

What job aspects have you enjoyed most so far ....
....
....

What do you do for recreation ....
....
....

Are you an active member of any clubs or social organisations ....
....

If this appointment is offered to you, when would you be able to start ...
....

I understand that if it is subsequently learnt that I have deliberately completed this form giving false information, then the Company reserves the right to take disciplinary action.

Signed .... Date ....

INTERVIEWERS' USE ONLY:

Assessment ....
....
....
....
....

Driving Licence checked ....

Salary agreed ....

Date of commencement ....

Area ....

Figure 5.4: HELIX standard application form

PRIVATE AND CONFIDENTIAL – APPLICATION AND PERSONAL RECORD

Position applied for ....

Would you work Full time? Yes/No   Part time Yes/No
If Part time, state hours
....

Surname .... Christian Names ....

Address ....

....

Tel. No ....

Age .... Date of Birth .... Nationality ....

Marital Status ....Number of Children Male .... Ages ....

Religion .... Female .... Ages ....

Next of Kin ....

Address of Next of Kin ....

Tel. No. of Next of Kin ....

Details of any qualifications or training. e.g. Apprenticeship,

First Aid etc. ....

....

....

Are you willing to work in any part of the factory if necessary ....

Have you ever suffered from any Industrial Disease? ....

Do you suffer from any disability and/or have you had any serious illness

or injury ....

Are you a registered disabled person ....

If yes, please give your Registration No. ....

Have you been employed by Helix International before ....

If yes, state date of leaving ....

Employment

Present/last employer ....

Type of business ....

Address ....

Occupation ....

Date from .... to .... Rate of pay ....

Reason you want to leave/have left ....

Please give details below of your previous employment, beginning with the most recent.

Employer .... Type of business ....

Address ....

Occupation ....

Date from .... to .... Rate of pay ....

Reason for leaving ....

Employer .... Type of business ....

Address ....

Occupation ....

Date from .... to .... Rate of pay ....

Reason for leaving ....

I accept that as and when the need arises I may be transferred from one department or job within the factory to another in accordance with Company directions.

I further accept that whilst every effort will be made to preserve my existing wage, such a transfer may result in a reduction of my pay.

I understand that if it is subsequently learned that I have deliberately completed this form giving false information, then the Company reserves the right to take disciplinary action.

I declare that the above is a true and accurate record and if this application is successful, I will abide by the company's Rules and Terms and Conditions of Employment.

Signature of Applicant .... Date ....

For Office Use Only

Interview comments ....

....

....

Engagement Instructions

To commence on	At .... a.m./p.m.
Shift	FT/PT ....
Occupation	Clock No. ....
Department	Rate of pay ....
N.I. No.	Full/Reduced Rate ....
Authority	Date ....

Figure 5.5: HELIX manual worker application form

If you decide to design your own application form, some guidelines follow (see Figure 5.6). It is not intended as a model, nor does your application form have to have each item. The best application forms will be those you design yourself, with the extensive knowledge you have of the company and the jobs for which they will be used. Use the guideline list as just that, a guide to your thinking.

Key points

1. Application forms filled in by candidates have a number of uses, including:
   - Screening applicants
   - Pointers for interview questions
   - Discovering the source of recruits
   - Public relations
   - Personnel records for successful candidates

2. They are useful even when applicants send you a CV.

3. Ideally, they are tailor made for a specific job, but two or three standard forms are adequate for most purposes.

4. The chapter includes five specimen application forms.

5. Typical topics to cover when constructing your own forms are:
   - Personal and family details
   - Education and training
   - Employment history
   - Job applied for
   - Candidate self-assessment
   - Names and addresses of referees

Subject	Examples of Items
Personal details	Name Address Telephone number Date of birth Marital status Race
Family background	Any relations employed by the company
Education and training	Schools/colleges attended Examinations passed Apprenticeships Professional qualifications Membership of professional societies, and grades
Employment history	Jobs in chronological order Nature of jobs Name and address of employer Salary at beginning and end Reason for leaving
Job applied for	Where heard about the job Date could start work Notice required by present employer Any previous application
Self-assessment	Career ambitions Work preferences
References	Names and addresses of work referees Whether free to contact them

Figure 5.6: Guidelines for application form items

6 Interviewing

'A bore is a man who, when you ask him how he is, tells you.'

Bert Leston Taylor

'One may smile and smile and be a villain.'

William Shakespeare

Why an Interview?

Whenever people consider picking people for jobs, the first thing they think of is interviewing. Hardly anyone is appointed to a job without being interviewed at some stage, often more than once. A recent survey of the popularity of different methods of selection showed that over 98% of employers use interviews.

The most popular method

Why is interviewing so popular? One attraction is that it gives you a 'feel' for the candidate. Nothing gives you this sense of getting to know the applicant better than chatting to her for half an hour. Also, you can assess aspects of that person which it is very difficult to assess by any other means; the way that she speaks, how neat her appearance, how well turned out, how relaxed and comfortable she is with other people, the list is endless.

Another good reason for its popularity is that recruiters believe that it works. Most people you speak to about selection think that the interview is a good method of getting to know someone. They think that they can make a good guess at whether they will be suitable for the job and the organization. Ask around. Ask yourself. Doesn't just about everyone feel that they can make a good shot at sussing someone at interview? Of course they do. After all, we are constantly making judgements about other people all day long, especially on first meeting. The interview is no different. It just involves meeting someone, having a chat and making up your mind what you think of them. Easy, isn't it?

I'm sorry to disillusion you, but the fact of the matter is that it's one of the weakest methods of selection. We can rate the effectiveness of different methods of predicting the performance of someone in a job on a scale from 0 to 100. Zero represents random selection – you'd make just as good a decision if you stuck a pin in a list of the candidates. One hundred means perfect prediction – right every single time. Interviews score way down at 15. Work samples and ability tests (which I'll come on to later) score much better at around 55.

Where's the evidence you say? How can I substantiate such a claim?

The answer lies in study after study, well designed and soberly analysed. These show that the unstructured interview, the one that you and I know and love, has a very low chance of picking the best person for the job. To use the jargon phrase, its predictive validity coefficient is close to zero. It just doesn't predict.

There is one classic example to illustrate the lack of agreement between inteviewers. Over fifty years ago, thirty-six candidates for the job of salesman were interviewed by six sales managers. There was very little agreement between interviewers on their ratings of the applicants for their suitability for the post. One candidate was rated first out of the thirty-six by one sales manager and last by another!

Why is the interview such a poor method?

There are lots of reasons why the typical interview has such a poor record as a predictive tool. (The typical interview, I said. All of them except yours, no doubt!) They include:

1. Most interviewers are not trained. Like many areas of management, people are often just thrust into the job of interviewing

when a vacancy needs to be filled. The need arises and they have to get on with it. Yet it is a skill that can be improved by training, just like any other.

2. Most people interview rarely, so they get very little practice. If the successful candidate turns out to be a flop, it is rarely assumed that the interview was to blame. This means that the interviewer hardly ever gets specific feedback on what she did wrong. So she never learns to do it right.

3. People often don't realize that they are bad at interviewing. There are three things that people always seem to think they are good at – driving a car, making love and interviewing. People believe that it is easy and natural. But there's lots of mistakes that can be made, and training and practice help. But if you don't think you need it, why bother to get trained?

4. The typical interview generates a lot of information. People find it very hard to separate out the important information from the unimportant. How important is it that a candidate is assertive, for example? One interviewer may see it as very important and so give it a lot of weight. Others see it as less important or even as irrelevant, and so don't let this trait influence their judgement.

5. Very importantly, selectors don't decide in a systematic way what skills, experience and qualities they are looking for in a candidate. They only rarely sit down and draw up a person specification as described in Chapter 2. So if they don't decide what they want in a candidate, it's not surprising that they make different decisions on different applicants.

6. Interviewers decide to accept or reject a candidate far too early in the interview, long before they have collected and considered all the evidence. A number of famous studies have shown that a typical interviewer makes up his or her mind about a candidate within the first four minutes of the interview. They then spend the rest of the interview finding evidence to support the decision they have already made. They seek out and remember good aspects of

the candidate if they have decided to accept her and negative aspects if they don't want to take her on.

7. Interviewers place more store by negative information than by positive evidence. It is almost as if they are looking for reasons for rejecting a candidate, and if they don't find any then she must be OK. This is obviously not ideal. What they should be doing is collecting information on whether the applicant can and will adequately do the job they have in mind.

8. Interviewers rarely change their minds about a candidate. Their minds are made up by the application form and initial appearances. What's the point of an interview if it doesn't add anything to initial impressions from application forms or prejudices based on physical appearance?

What's the purpose of the interview?

Let's look on the bright side. The interview may be a poor predictor of job performance, but it does serve some useful purposes. These are:

1. It allows you to meet the candidate. At least you will know what she looks like when she arrives for work on the first day! More seriously, it allows you to attempt to assess things like whether she is smartly turned out and able to communicate orally.

But *beware*! Meeting the candidate lays the poor interviewer open to all the prejudices and biases that so many of us are familiar with. Perhaps in a few jobs, where the person has to deal with members of the public, such as banks, building societies, shops, etc, a smart appearance is an important requirement. But in many jobs ask yourself a simple question. Does the fact that he has long hair really matter? Or that her race or gender is different from yours? Or that he wears suede shoes or has a beard? Always subject your instant reactions and snap judgements to the discipline of asking yourself if it truly affects the successful performance of this job that the person looks or behaves like she does.

2. It allows the candidate to meet you. In particular, it lets her find out about the job and the organization. She can meet the people she will be working with and get the feel of the buildings or environment in which she will work.

3. It gives the candidate the feeling that she has been given a fair crack of the whip. If you turn her down, at least she feels she had a chance to get the job.

All is not lost: making a poor method better

Despite the poor showing of the interview in the typical amount of agreement there is between interviewers, and its poor record at getting the best candidate, all is not lost. There are ways of making this shaky method rather better. But I would never advise that you rely on the interview as the sole means of assessing someone for a job. Always supplement it with some of the other methods described in this book. That way, you will give yourself a much better chance of spotting the best candidate for you.

A guide to effective interviewing

There are a number of tips and techniques which can help turn you into a better interviewer. They are:

- Have a plan
- Develop rapport
- Take notes
- Use lots of open questions to get the candidate talking
- Use closed questions to probe for specific points of information
- Don't ask leading questions
- Make sure that the candidate talks more than you do
- Avoid prejudice and bias
- Only ask relevant questions

Have a plan	It is best to have a structure to the interview, outline it to the candidate, and follow it yourself
Develop rapport	Be natural and friendly with the candidates. Make them feel relaxed so that their behaviour is natural
Take notes	Notes help you remember what was said. Keep them short to avoid lengthy breaks in eye contact
Open and closed questions	Use open questions to obtain a general picture. Use closed questions to probe.
Leading questions	Make sure that the way questions are asked does not tell the candidate the reply to give
Talking time	The purpose of the interview is to provide you with information on the candidate. Therefore he or she should talk 75% of the time, you only 25%
Prejudice and bias	Your judgement of the candidate should depend on the facts, not on bias
Relevance	The content of the interview should provide relevant information on whether the candidate is suitable for the job

Table 6.1 A Guide to effective interviewing

A summary of these key points of conducting interviews is contained in Table 6.1.

1. *Have a plan*

There is a lot to be said for having a structure or a plan for your interview. It helps you cover the main points and not miss out crucial areas. There are lots of recommended plans around. One simple one splits the interview into three stages, a beginning, a middle and an end. This is shown in Table 6.2.

Interview stage	Objectives	Activities
Beginning	Put candidate at ease Develop rapport Set the scene	Greet candidate by name Introduce self Neutral chat Agree interview purpose Outline how purpose will be achieved
Middle	Collect and give information Maintain rapport	Ask questions within a structure Listening Observation Answering questions
End	Close interview Confirm future action	Summarize interview Check candidate has no more questions Say what happens next

Table 6.2 A Simple Interview Plan
Adapted from: Torrington and Hall (1987).

The straightforward plan in Table 6.2 is useful to make sure that you have covered most of the important areas in the interview. The only piece of advice in the list which may need explaining is the phrase 'Ask questions within a structure'. The structure could be a biographical one, i.e. based on a candidate's background and experiences. You can choose to take it forward or backwards in time. So you could start with questions about schooling, followed by first job, second job, third job, and so on. Or you could start the other way round, with the most recent job, followed by the one before that and the one before that, and so on. Obviously, the older and more experienced a person is, the less time and emphasis you are going to want to place on early experiences. They are less relevant now that they are so far in the past. This allows you more time on the recent achievements.

Another structure you could adopt is not based on the sequence of experiences of a person but upon areas that you are interested in. So there might first be a whole series of questions on education, then on work, then on training, and so on.

Other well-known structures are the five-, seven- or eight-point plans which I described in Chapter 3, and you used in Chapter 4. You can gather information about the candidate under the headings used in the plans.

The key point it, whatever structure you adopt, it must be logical. There is no need to stick to it religiously. You can be flexible, so as to cope with inevitable differences between people. But it should be a plan that guides each and every interview, so that information is gathered systematically on every important area for each candidate.

It is always best to agree the interview structure with the candidate at the beginning. You might say something like: 'What I want to do in the next hour or so, Ms Candidate, is firstly to ask you some questions about why you want to come and work here. Next I'd like to talk to you about the jobs you have had in the past, discuss your education and training, and find out a little about what you do outside of work. Then I'll try to describe the company and job, and answer any questions you have about them. Is that OK with you?'

The advantage of setting out the structure for the candidate in this way is that she then has a framework or guide so that she knows what will happen. She knows what will be talked about and roughly when. She can relate your questions to the framework, so that they become part of a logical whole rather than a disjointed shopping list of questions.

It also enables you to control the meeting. You can steer the conversation on to the next area by saying: 'Now I'd like to move on to the topic of your education . . .'

2. *Develop rapport*

Remember that you want to get to know the candidate. Even an experienced candidate is likely to be nervous, so do your best to put her at ease. Offer her a cup of tea or coffee. Show her around the site. Arrange the furniture so as not to intimidate. Offer her a comfortable chair. Talk about neutral subjects at the start such as:

How was the journey here?
Have you come far?
Do you know this part of the world at all?
(Even, if you must) . . . Hasn't it been wet for the time of year?

Use body language to help you. Try to remember SOLER. This stands for:

Square Open Lean Eye-contact Relax

- Face the candidate *Squarely*. Don't look out of the window, continually at your papers, or half way round in your chair.

- Have an *Open* body posture. This means without folded hands, bent head, hunched up or hostile, threatening and suspicious-looking!

- *Lean* forward (though not so much that you are in their lap!) to show interest in what they are saying. Especially, lean forward slightly when the candidate is saying something your are particularly keen to hear about, or when you want to take control.

- Maintain *Eye-contact*. Look at the candidate. Don't overdo this, though, and stare them out. Nod, to encourage them to talk.

- Try to *Relax*. If you are, candidates will pick this up, and it will help them to relax. There is nothing worse for an interview*ee* than a nervous, self-conscious interview*er*.

3. *Take notes*
All the time, you should be questioning, probing, observing and making notes. You might think that note taking will get in the way of rapport. There is certainly a danger of this. It does force you to break off eye contact and can distract you from what the interviewee is saying. But if you keep the notes short, the risk is minimal. If you don't like taking notes at the time, write them up immediately afterwards. Bear in mind that you will have a number of interviews to conduct, probably separated by some days. You'll want to refer to the interview after you have seen all the

candidates in order to make up your mind on the best. Without notes you are relying on memory, which can easily let you down.

4. *Open and closed questions*

The purpose of the interview is for you to find out about the candidate, especially whether she is capable of doing a good job for you. Therefore a key feature of your questions should be to give her a chance to talk. Particularly at the early stages of the interview, you should use open questions.

Open questions are those that get the candidate talking. Examples are:

Tell me about your present job.
This new system you put in, tell me about it.
You say you feel stifled by your present job. Why is that?
What problems do you think you might have adapting to our way of doing things here?

Their common feature is that they cannot be answered with a short answer like 'yes' or 'no'.

Closed questions are those that require only a few words to answer them. Examples are:

How long were you with Smith and Jones Ltd?
Are you happy to work the occasional weekend?
Do you know how many direct competitors we have?
Have you ever been in business on your own?
Do you have a company car?

These questions don't usually get the candidate talking. So you should avoid them, especially at the beginning of an interview. You may find them valuable occasionally to probe a particular point or to clear up a specific issue, like 'How much notice do you have to give to your present employer', but you should keep them to a minimum. You can usually find most of this kind of information in the application form anyway.

It is usually fairly easy to rephrase closed into open ones, with the benefit of getting much more information. For example:

Closed: How long were you with Smith and Jones Ltd?
Open: Tell me about your time at Smith and Jones Ltd.
Closed: Are you happy working at weekends?
Open: How would you feel about working unsocial hours?
Closed: Do you know how many direct competitors we have?
Open: What do you know of our competitors?

5. *Leading questions*

Leading questions are those that give the answer the interviewer is looking for in the question. The candidate will almost certainly oblige by giving you just the answer she knows you are looking for. They are not to be recommended simply because they tell you nothing. Take a look at the closed questions in section 3 above. How many of them are also leading questions?

Other examples are:

You have got experience of working with engineers, haven't you?
Wouldn't you say that the government is making a great mistake in privatizing public utilities?
If you were appointed, you wouldn't mind teaching this course, would you?

It is a brave, unusually honest or foolish interviewee who doesn't accept and agree with the answer so waiting to be agreed with. The last example was one I was asked at a university appointments board interview. Wanting the job, I readily agreed, even though I knew very little about the course in question. I never did teach it, even though appointed. How much more sensible it would have been to have asked an open and non-leading question like 'If asked to teach this course, what sorts of material would you want to cover in it?' That would have instantly displayed my ignorance!

Other re-writes of leading questions are:

Leading: You have got experience of working with engineers, haven't you?

Non-leading:	Can you tell me about any experience you have had working with engineers?
Leading:	Wouldn't you say that the government is making a great mistake in privatizing public utilities?
Non-leading:	What do you feel about the government's privatization programme?

6. *Talking time*

Remember that a key aim of the interview is for you to find out about the candidate. So don't use the whole interview telling her what a wonderful place your organization is in which to work, and how much fun you are to work with. Ask open questions to get her talking and then listen, observe and take brief notes. Steer the conversation into areas you need to know about. Keep a firm grip on the structure, coming back to it if you go off down an interesting and important side alley. But keep mum for a large part of the time. Aim to get the candidate talking for about 75% of the time.

By all means leave ample time at the end of the interview for the candidate to ask questions. Show her around the site and invite questions. But during the bulk of the interview, question and probe. Above all, listen. We were born with two ears and one mouth. Try to use them in that proportion.

7. *Prejudice and bias*

I'd like you to take a break here. Take a look at the sheet on the next page. It asks you to note down any beliefs you have about what makes a good employee in your organization, and any types of people you don't like working with. Do it now.

Now take a look to see how many of them you can honestly justify as necessary for the job. Put a tick in the Necessary column. Aren't the rest really subjective biases or prejudices? If so, watch out the next time you select.

Table 6.4 shows a list of typical subjectivities in selection. Have you, like me, heard these?

Remember, your judgement of the candidate should be based on the facts, not on your biases.

Please note down on this form:

1. Any characteristics you think make a good employee where you work.

2. Any characteristics that make an unacceptable employee where you work.

3. Any types of people with whom you don't like working.

4. When you have done 1–3, take a backward step and think to yourself:

How really necessary are these statements to effective performance?

Are they fair?

Could I justify them in objective, factual terms, e.g. by providing data to support the good and bad peformers, or are they just based on one or two individuals? Worse, are they in truth based on bias?

5. Then take a look at the next table of typical biases and subjective judgements. Did you have any the same?

CHARACTERISTICS OF:

Good Employees	Poor Employees	People I don't like working with	Necessary?

Table 6.3 Record Sheet

8. *Relevance*

It is important always to ask questions which are relevant to the job on offer, rather than just ramble over issues which you find interesting. Too many interviewers in my experience just don't

Each of the following biases and subjective judgements I have heard said, at one time or another, by people selecting others:

'We don't let people with beards work here.'

'No self-respecting man ever wears a brown suit.'

'I can tell before they take a seat if they are right for the job. It's the brisk, determined walk I look for.'

'A firm handshake. That tells you a lot about someone.'

'I reject people who have spelling mistakes in their application forms.'

'I won't have a nanny who shaves her legs looking after my children.'

'I couldn't work with someone with ginger hair.'

'We mostly only recruit graduates from Oxbridge.'*

'Salesmen here have got to be over 6 feet tall.'

'I watch out for people with moist hands. You can't trust them.'

'First I look at their hands. People who bite their finger nails are neurotic and won't cope with pressure.'

'Suede shoes aren't allowed.'

'We reject people who hand-write their application forms.'

'We reject people who type their application forms.'

* Tempting reply: So did the British Secret Service. Look where that got them.

Think how tough it must be if you're a 5 foot 6 inch Cambridge scholar, with a beard and sweaty palms, who looks good in brown suits!

Table 6.4 Subjectivity in Selection

know what to say in an interview. So they resort to talking about things that *they* know about or are interested in. Many are the interviewers who have talked about golf, the state of the economy, or the government of the day. These may serve as a brief opening to settle the candidate down, especially neutral subjects like the weather or the ease of parking in the area. But they should not occupy much time. The fact that they often do is a sure sign that the interviewer is inexperienced or just plain bad at the job in hand.

So remember the following:

- Prepare questions in advance.
- Always ask questions that are related to the person specification, i.e. that are job relevant.
- Note down how satisfactory you think the answers are. That way you have a comparison when you see the next candidate, which might be some days away.

Types of interview

Assuming that you decide to conduct an interview, what are the different types of interview that you can consider? Three old favourites are the:

- Board (or panel) interview
- Individual interview
- Sequential interview

There are also the:

- Stress interview
- Situational interview

Let's look at each type in turn.

1. *The board interview*

This is where a number of interviewers, comprising a board or panel, meet to interview candidates. It is common in the public sector, especially for teaching appointments.

On the face of it, a board interview seems to have little in its favour. It is often intimidating to the candidate, who has to face a row of interviewers and a barrage of questions. It is very difficult to establish rapport, even if the board comprises just two or three people. I once saw a board of fourteen! The research evidence indicates that, while boards don't necessarily make worse decisions than individual interviews, they don't make better ones either. Finally, they are difficult to manage. Board members have the bother of dealing with one another as well as with the candidate. They have to decide how they will allocate questions among themselves, who will chair and how the final decision will be reached. Such problems are less acute in individual interviews.

Supporters of the method can point to some advantages, though.

(a) It is claimed that panels reduce bias in decision-making. This may well be the case. It is less easy to appoint or not appoint on such discriminatory bases as race, gender or nepotism when the decision has to be shared among others who were present at the interview.

(b) Board interviews also exist for political reasons. There are often lots of interested parties to the selection and each must play a part in the decision. Sometimes it is compulsory to invite holders of certain posts to take part in the interview. The question is not who should be there, but which posts should be represented. The classic case is in school teacher appointments. Here the employer (the Local Authority) often insists that the Head Teacher, the Chair of the Board of Governors, the Local Authority representative (such as the Inspector for the subject to be taught) and at least two members of the Authority's Education committee, be members of the interview panel.

The best advice that can be given if political considerations make it necessary for a board to be convened is to make sure that it functions well. This means that there should be an agreed chairperson. Members of the panel should be clear beforehand on the role they are to play, especially which topics they are expected to cover with the candidate. Finally, make sure that no one person dominates. If one person is obviously higher status than the others, there is always a tendency for that person to influence the decision of all the other members. If that happens, the board loses its advantage of reducing bias, and it means that all it gains is the extra expense of many people's time being wasted.

2. *The individual interview*
This is the interview most of us think of when the topic is mentioned. It involves just one person interviewing a candidate or series of candidates. Here, the advantages and disadvantages of the board interview are reversed. It has lots of potential for bias. On the other hand, it does allow the good interviewer to establish rapport. And it allows you to probe into important areas of the candidate's experience without feeling that you must pass the questioning on to another board member.

3. *The sequential interview*
As the name suggests, this is where there are a sequence of interviews of one candidate, but conducted by different people. It has many of the advantages of both the board and the individual interview. It is the best of the interview methods. It allows you to establish rapport and get to know the candidate in a relaxed, relatively informal way. Because a number of interviewers are involved, each making up their mind independently, it helps prevent bias.

It still means that a group decision has to be reached, though. The outcome can still be swayed by the most influential rather than the best judge of the candidate's suitability. This is something that should be guarded against. A matrix method, like the one I recommended in Chapter 4, can help. So does giving each interviewer the task of finding out about one major aspect of the candidate, agreed in advance. It could be one of the eight points from the eight-point plan. That way, all interviewers have a chance of being heard at the wrap-up session. But it isn't foolproof.

4. *Stress interviews*
You may have heard of stress interviews. The view is sometimes put forward that the job is stressful and so the interviewer needs to find out if the candidate can cope with stress. In these cases, the inteviewer aims at being rude or abusive to the candidate. Or asking impossible questions and then being hostile about the answer. Most experienced interviewers do not resort to so-called stress interviews for a number of reasons, the most important

one being that it breaks any rapport that might have been established. Also, it is highly likely that more interviewees will be rejected than accepted. Those who are not selected will take away a very negative view of the inteviewer and, by implication, the organization. The interviewer has a duty to her organization to keep the public relations element of the interview in mind. No organization wants disgruntled, failed candidates going around grumbling about the arrogant, high-handed interview methods it adopts. This is particularly important in times of shortage of key candidates.

If you want to find out if the candidate can cope with stress, then being rude in the interview is not likely to give you the answer. All it really tells you is if she can cope with rude interviewers! Instead, ask the candidate to give you examples of stress at work that she has had to deal with. Probe specifically how she coped. Or try to find this out from previous employers by following up references.

5. *Situational interviews*

Recently, a new form of interview has been developed, called the situational interview. In some respects it is like the hypothetical question sometimes asked in conventional interviews. Candidates are asked to say what they would do in certain situations.

One difference, though, is in the origin of the question. In the ordinary: 'What would you do if . . .?' type of question, the interviewer is usually just making up an example from her own head. A candidate for the job of policeman might be asked: 'Suppose you are alone in an inner-city area and you pass a pub. Someone rushes out and says that there is a fight going on inside. What would you do?'

The question may seem sensible but has a number of problems with it. The main one is, is this a realistic question? In other words, does it really happen with any regularity?

In the situational interview, the interviewer only asks 'situational' questions that she knows are realistic and appropriate. She knows this from critical incident job analysis (see Chapter 2). This has shown that the event does occur regularly enough to make the question sensible. And there will be a series of such situational questions, not just one.

A second difference is in how the reply is coded. In the situational interview, the questioner has a number of standard replies. Each is graded according to its appropriateness. So if a candidate replied: 'I'd go in and sort them out' or 'I'd run away and climb a tree', she would get a low score. If she said: 'I'd radio for help', she'd get a better one. Again, the responses are coded based on research, this time according to what effective police officers do, when compared with less effective ones.

You can see that the interview is highly structured and the ratings made by the interviewer are standardized. Such methods make for better reliability. Yet such pre-designed questions and pre-coded answers don't need to be asked face to face. There is no reason why you couldn't ask the questions in a written test, if you choose, saving you time. The true interview can be left to provide information to the candidate on the job and the organization. Or to fulfil the ritual so expected by both parties.

Situational interviews are a very good idea, and have a lot to recommend them. But in many ways they are more like tests than interviews.

It is to the use of tests in selection that we turn next.

Key points

1. Interviewing is an extremely popular selection method, despite its poor record of predicting the work performance of candidates.

2. Interviews are a chance for you to meet the candidate, and for the candidate to find out about you, the job and the organization.

3. They also provide lots of opportunity for subjectivity and irrelevant biases to creep into your judgement of the applicant.

4. Simple rules of thumb can help you avoid the worst pitfalls, like:

   - Have a plan
   - Develop rapport
   - Use open questions
   - Avoid leading questions

5. There is a choice of different types of interview. They are:

   - Board (or panel)
   - Individual
   - Sequential
   - Situational

6. Stress interviews should be avoided.

7 References

'When I want to understand what is happening today or try to decide what will happen tomorrow, I look back.'

Oliver Wendell Holmes

'Beware of false knowledge; it is more dangerous than ignorance.'

George Bernard Shaw

Occupational psychologists (social scientists who study people at work) are usually very negative about references. They will cite you study after study which shows the poor reliability and validity of the method. Just a few studies show that they are useful in certain circumstances. Most show them to be one of the poorer selection methods – about as bad as the interview, which, as you now know, is also frowned upon for its unreliability.

And yet . . . and yet. If current selection practice is anything to go by, recruiters love references. A recent survey showed that two thirds of major British employers always take them up. Only a handful never do. Think about it yourself. Don't you normally take up references? Aren't you often asked to write references for others? I know I am. I'm pestered by the things.

So again, we find that relatively poor methods are used extensively. Why?

Why use references?

References have lots of apparent advantages.

1. They are cheap. It only takes one letter and a few stamps to send out a whole batch. Other people spend their time on

assessing your candidates, without pay. That has got to be a good deal! And phone references don't take much more time and money.

2. You can use references to verify factual information. Has the candidate been telling the truth in the interview? Has he filled out the application form accurately, or has he (to be kind) stretched a point or two. It is not at all uncommon to find that an assistant to the Assistant Deputy Branch Manager of a small regional office gets promoted to the Regional Manager in the time it takes to write out an application form. Or that his salary takes on a similar sudden hike when he's asked on the application form to give his earnings in his present post. Specific information like this can be verified by referees.

3. You can use them to find out a different sort of information – what the candidate is like. The interview lets the candidate speak about himself. The reference lets someone else speak about him. You can ask a whole series of questions. What is he like? How does he deal with customers? Does he have a drink problem which interferes with his work? Does he have any major weaknesses? Where do his strengths lie? Why did he leave his previous jobs? I know one Sales Director who regularly rings up referees and grills them for more than half an hour about a candidate he is interested in. What he's after is just this sort of valuable 'soft' data which is difficult to get in any other way.

Unfortunately, woolly, unfocused, written appraisals are seldom useful, as I will explain in a moment.

What types of reference are there?

So, references have the aim of finding out about someone from someone else. There are lots of sources of this information, some better than others. Some of the main ones are:

- Testimonials, or letters of recommendation
- Personal referees
- Schools, colleges, universities and examination boards

- Written references from previous employers
- Telephone references from employers

I'll take each in turn.

1. *Testimonials*
Testimonials are the sort of piece of paper which begins 'To Whom it may Concern'. They used to be popular, and, in my experience, still are in certain parts of the world. They are much less common in Britain now. They have little practical use. If the testimonial was at all negative, you can be sure that the candidate would have burnt it long ago. They tend to be full of glowing phrases or else glib platitudes, of little worth. And they are so easy to forge. I recommend you ignore them.

2. *Personal references*
These are still asked for by employers. They are like the passport application that asks for it to be signed by a vicar, a doctor, or some other such worthy. When used for job applications they're usually one of a number of other references the applicant is asked to provide. They suffer from the same problem as the testimonial. Who is going to present a reference from someone who says negative things about them? Would you, in their place? Forget them.

3. *Examination boards and educational references*
These can be useful if the qualifications of the candidate are crucial to effective performance on the job. In such cases it is a good idea to write to the college, polytechnic, or whatever, and asks them to verify that Jill Smith was there between the dates she says she was, and did obtain the qualification in veterinary science or interior design she claims she got.

Whether you should write or ring them to find out about the individual's personality is covered next.

4. *Written references*
This is not a satisfactory method, and it explains much of the criticism stemming from scientific work on the value of the

reference. Letters from referees have lots wrong with them. In case you are tempted to waste your time and other people's in this ritual dance, let's look at the sources of error.

One problem is that people often don't know well enough the people they are asked to comment on. A teacher, particularly at an institute of higher education like a university, may have hundreds of students in the class and see the group just ten hours a year for one topic. The lecturer can't possibly know everyone well.

When I used to be an external assessor for the Civil Service Selection Board, I remember one senior civil servant telling me that he had been involved for a number of years with reading headteacher references. He had seen thousands of them, every single one favourable, mostly glowingly so. Then one time he got a negative reference on a candidate. He was delighted. Such a change! On interviewing the pupil later, he discovered that the headteacher had made a mistake. He had mixed up the candidate with another boy with a similar name. He never did get to meet the origin of the only negative reference he ever received. How many times do such mix-ups happen without you or I discovering the error, I wonder?

Even if we know someone, some people just aren't good at describing others. The blank sheet of paper type of reference relies on our powers of description.

Mostly, though, the reference is limited as a source of information because employers don't want to be critical of someone, especially given the laws of libel and the fact that the reference might not be treated confidentially. A candidate's present employer may be especially nice about just the person you want to find out about most – the poor performer. If such a person at last decides to leave his job, is his boss going to give him a bad reference? Certainly not. This is just the chance the employer has been looking for. So he gives no grounds for concern to you, the prospective next employer, who might just be foolish enough to take his burden from him.

If you must write rather than phone, always send a checklist, not a blank sheet of paper. Some example questions are shown in Table 7.1. The specific questions on your own list will depend on

Poor postal reference questions (if this is all you use)

Please give your impression of this candidate's ability, character and personality

or

Please say what the candidate is like as an employee

or

Do you consider the candidate suitable for the job she/he has applied for with us?

Note: These are poor because they are so vague. They are very unlikely to give you specific or negative information. In particular, they may well tell you nothing about the key characteristics you know you need in the successful candidate, based on your person specification for the job

Some better postal reference questions

Please give dates on which the candidate entered and left school/ college/university/ the armed forces/your employment/etc
Please give the reasons the person left
Was the person's health satisfactory?
What was the person's attendance record? How many periods of absence did he/she have?
How was the person's time keeping? How many times was the person late for work?
. . . and so on . . . See the telephone reference checklist for other specific questions

Table 7.1 Postal Reference Questions

the essential and desirable candidate qualities you identified in the person specification (see Chapter 2). The checklist can be very similar to a telephone reference form, which I'm coming on to in a moment. It can also incude a rating scale, though most research, and my own experience, shows that the negative end of the scale hardly ever gets used.

5. *Telephone reference*

This is the best form of reference check. They should be used *before* you interview the shortlisted candidates. That way, you can see if you still want them on the shortlist. It might also throw up areas of concern which you can probe in the interview.

Never approach previous employers if the candidate asks you not to. Nor should you contact the present employer if they don't know that the candidate is looking for another job.

- *What is the best way of getting a telephone reference?*

By far the best way is to have a ready-prepared checklist of questions. Remember the two main purposes of the reference. One is to verify the information you already have from the application form or the first interview. The second is to tease out information about what the individual is like as a person.
So structure the reference conversation that way. Ask questions of a factual nature first. Then go on to ask about the candidate's personality. Take notes during the conversation.
The conversation might go something like this:

- *Introduction*

Ms Candidate has applied for a position with this firm. Do you remember her? Would you verify some of the information she has given us?

- *Questions to verify information*

She states that she was employed by you between these dates. Is that correct?
What post did she hold when she started with you?
What post did she hold when she left?
Do you know her pay at the time? What proportion was bonus (commission, incentive, etc)?
She says she left because . . . Is this true?

- *Some examples of questions about the person*

How good was her attendance?
How good was her time-keeping?
Did she have any habits which affected her work (e.g. drinking, gambling)?
How much was she supervised?
How hard did she work?

How did she get on with colleagues?
How did she get on with superiors?
How did she get on with subordinates?
Where were her strengths?
What were her weak points?
Would you reappoint her?

Table 7.2 shows a typical telephone reference checklist used by an office products company.

Naturally, when you have the information, all you have is one person's view. It is always advisable to get a minimum of three different people who know a candidate's work. References often say more about the author than about the candidate. An interesting study of medical school applicants showed this can be true. One reference on a candidate rarely agreed with what was written about the same candidate by someone else. But references written about different candidates by the *same* person did say the same thing! This suggests that each referee had a characteristic way of writing a reference, saying similar things about different people.

So beware! Get more than one reference. Treat them with caution.

Key points

1. References have a very poor reliability and validity record; they are weak predictors of job performance.

2. They have the advantage that they are cheap.

3. They can be used to:

    - Verify factual information (sometimes useful)
    - Gather impressions (very rarely useful)

4. There are many types of reference. These include:

Name of shortlisted applicant: ______________________

Person contacted for reference: ______________ **Position:** ______________

Company: ______________________ **Tel. No:** ______________

1. Did he report directly to you? ______	Right Person?	Yes/No
2. What were the dates of employment with your company? From: ______ To: ______	Do dates check?	Yes No
3. What was his basic salary? ______ p.a.	Did he falsify?	Yes/No
4. Monthly commission average or bonuses? ______	Did he exaggerate?	Yes/No
5. Did he have a company car? Yes/No. Type ______	Did he exaggerate?	Yes/No
6. What other benefits did he receive?	Petrol/WPA/Telephone Etc.	
7. What was his attendance record? ______	Conscientious?	Yes/No
	Health	Good/Bad
8. What kind of work did he do? ______	Misrepresentation?	Yes/No
9. Was his paperwork/administration accurate, on time?	Problems Admin.?	Yes/No
10. How did his work results compare with others? ______	Competitive?	
11. Was he tenacious? ______		
12. How closely was he supervised? ______	Industrious?	Yes/No
13. Does he meet objectives/deadlines? ______		Yes/No
14. His relationship with colleagues? ______	Troublemaker?	
15. His relationship with customers? ______	Company image?	
16. Did he have any health problems? ______	Health affected?	Yes/No
17. Was he an excessive drinker? ______	Reliability?	
18. Did he experience financial difficulties or have any domestic problems? ______	Immaturity? Work affected?	
19. Did any outside interests impact on work? ______		
Was he an honest person? ______	Expenses? Misleader?	
21. Was he accurate and reliable? ______	Attention to detail?	
22. Did he supervise ______ How many? ______	Does this check?	
If 'Yes' how well did he manage? ______	Good Man Manager? Leader or Driver?	
23. What are his strengths? ______		
24. What are his weaknesses? ______	Related to Job/Personal?	
25. What were his specific skills/experience ______		
26. What did you think of him? ______	Hard to manage?	
27. Why did he leave? ______	Do reasons check?	
28. Where was he working prior to joining your company? ______	Does this check?	
29. Who did he join when he left you? ______	Does this check?	

30. Would you re hire him? ______ If not, why not? ______________________

31. Any problems that I should know about? ______________________

32. Could you verify his specific qualifications? ______________________

Signed: ______________________ Date: ______________

Table 7.2 Telephone reference checklist

- Testimonials
- Personal
- Educational
- Written
- Telephone

Telephone references, along with verification of educational qualifications in certain circumstances, are better methods than the rest.

5. If you feel you must use references, get more than one per applicant.

6. Treat other people's views of your candidates with a healthy degree of scepticism.

8 Testing

> 'There's one way to find out if a man is honest – ask him. If he says 'Yes' you know he is a crook.'
>
> *Groucho Marx*

> 'Everybody is ignorant, only on different subjects.'
>
> *Will Rogers*

Testing as an aid to picking the right person for a job is increasing in popularity, although a full testing programme is mainly reserved for more senior jobs. The reason for the increasing interest no doubt lies in the increasing importance of getting the decision right, as we discussed in Chapter 1. So anything which can help the decision-making process is worth a try even if it costs rather more than traditional methods. This obviously begs the question of whether tests in fact *do* help us to make better decisions. We will look at the issue in this chapter. But first, just what are tests and what sorts are available?

What are tests?

Tests have been used to select people for thousands of years. Take a look at Box 1 for an example of an early use of a test to select soldiers.

Tests and questionnaires used in selection have traditionally been paper and pencil instruments which are filled out by the candidate, and then scored and interpreted by the person doing the testing. In recent years the paper and pencil style of testing has given way to automated methods. Here the instrument is 'administered' (that is, presented to the candidate) on a microcomputer screen. Then, at

BOX 1

An Early Use of Selection Testing

Behavioural tests have been used for at least 3000 years. One was used by Gideon to choose 300 men from his army of 32,000 to fight the Mid'ianites.

> And the LORD said to Gideon, 'The people are still too many; take them down to the water and I will test them for you there; and he of whom I say to you, 'This man shall go with you', shall go with you; and any of whom I say to you, 'This man shall not go with you', shall not go.' So he brought the people down to the water; and the LORD said to Gideon, 'Every one that laps the water with his tongue, as a dog laps, you shall set by himself; likewise every one that kneels down to drink.' And the number of those that lapped, putting their hands to their mouths, was three hundred men; but all the rest of the people knelt down to drink water. And the LORD said to Gideon, 'With the three hundred men that lapped, I will deliver you, and give the Mid'ianites into your hand; and let all the others go every man to his home.' *Judges* 7, 4–7

May, H. G. and Metzger, G. M. (eds) *The New Oxford Annotated Bible*, Revised Standard Version. New York, Oxford University Press, pp. 302–3, 1973.

the touch of a button, the instrument is scored and statistics, profile sheets and descriptions of the person tested are printed off. Quite obviously, this saves a lot of time and hassle for the tester, but only really makes economic sense if you have a large number of candidates and a desktop computer already available.

Tests aim to give a picture of the applicant. You then compare this with other information on that candidate that you get from the interview or application form. It can also be compared with other candidates, or perhaps with a profile of an 'ideal' candidate. Tests and questionnaires have usually been designed by psychologist, but you don't need to be a psychologist to use them.

Are tests and questionnaires the same thing?

Strictly speaking, there are two broad sorts of tests. One group can fairly be described as tests while the other sort are better called questionnaires. The difference is that tests are those instruments where you usually have a time limit and, more importantly, have one right answer. They are designed to measure abilities or skills, such as mental arithmetic, thinking ability or typing skill, and try to test how accurate, bright, or skilful you are.

Questionnaires, on the other hand, are more often used to measure personality or interests. They are not timed and only have a 'right answer' in the sense that it describes an applicant. So, a question like 'I usually find it quite easy to argue my side of the case in a meeting' has no absolute right or wrong answer. It is only true or not true of the person completing the questionnaire.

Although what I have just said about the differences between tests and questionnaires is true, it's a bit nit-picking. Psychologists like to point out the semantic difference but, in everyday use, most people just call them tests. I will do so here. The term 'psychometric test' is sometimes used by those in the know. The 'metric' part of the word refers to measurement, while the 'psycho' or pschological part of the word means you and your behaviour.

Types of test

There are three broad categories of tests which are used in picking people for jobs. These are:

- General mental ability
- Specific aptitudes and ability
- Personality

Interest questionnaires are occasionally used as well. They look at the sorts of interests a person has, such as working with people or pursuing an artistic career. They are commonly used when someone is wanting advice on which occupation or training course is likely to suit their interests. They have only limited use in personnel selection because they rely so much on the candidate being honest about their interests. In a selection situation it is so easy to give the tester the answer which you feel will go down well, regardless of its truth. In fact, this is also a problem for personality questionnaires and interviews, but it doesn't stop their use!

1. *Mental ability tests*

Once upon a time every school child did the 11-plus exam. Maybe you did it. If so, you will remember a specific type of mental ability test – the *intelligence test*. It usually consisted of numbers, words and shapes and you were expected to continue a sequence or spot the odd one out. Opposite is an example of this type of test.

These tests usually call on three types of reasoning – verbal, numerical and spatial. So items designed to measure each part involve words, numbers or shapes. It is easy to assume that some occupations require one form of ability rather than another. For example, we expect writers or teachers to be good with words, accountants to be better at numbers, and architects to be more skilled at reasoning with diagrams and shapes. But research shows what many of us suspected all along, which is that it's not a fair world. When these sorts of abilities were being given out, some people were given a greater share than others. So while you may be better at one sort of item than another (better at words than at figures, for example), the truth of the matter is that if you are good at one set, the chances are that you will be good at them all, relative to other people. And the opposite holds true. If you find, say, the verbal items difficult, the chances are that you will find all three categories of item relatively difficult.

So, if you have a job that needs someone to reason and think quickly in an abstract way, or learn new things, tests are a very useful way of assessing this. This applies, whatever the level or type of job.

Tests of general intelligence or IQ are still used in selection, although they have been largely overtaken at senior levels of jobs by more specific and less abstract thinking and reasoning tests. They aim to measure the capacity for abstract thinking and reasoning. Scores on the tests are designed to relate to the individual's capacity to learn or perform a new skill, rather than their existing level. It was for this reason that they were used as a

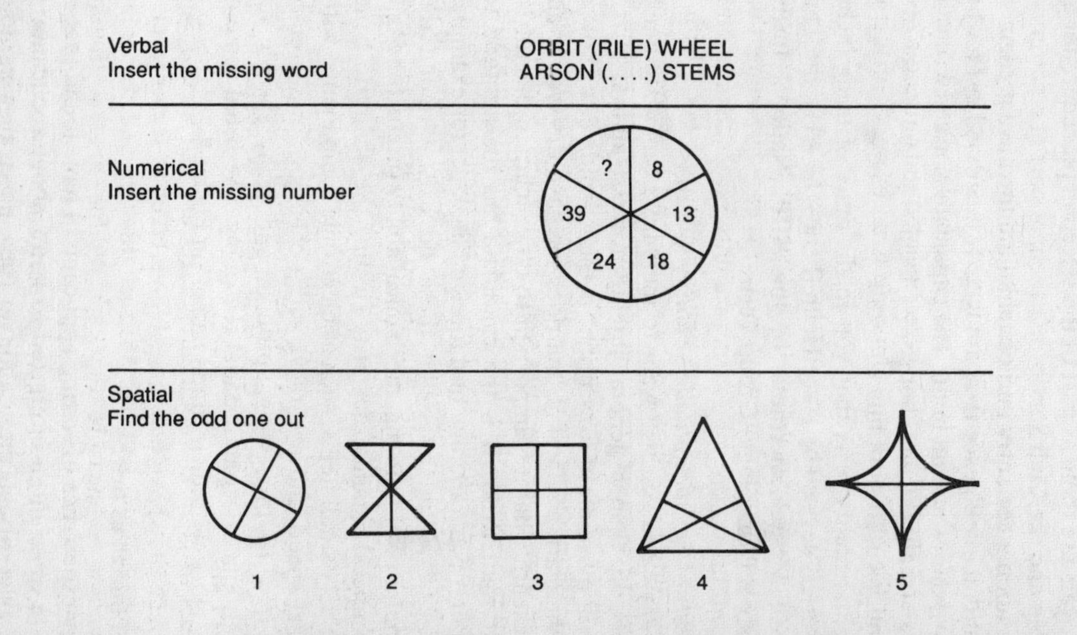

Figure 8.1: Examples of typical items from classical intelligence tests

screen or filter for the type of further education a school child was allowed to enter. Intelligence tests are useful for testing large numbers of people at once, say when a dozen or more individuals have applied for the same job or group of jobs. Many large employers use them as part of the selection procedure for apprenticeship and the Civil Service use them as part of a battery of tests and exercises for entry into certain administrative grades.

General intelligence tests are usually timed and last for between thirty minutes and an hour. The candidate is asked to choose one answer (the right one, hopefully) from among a range of five or six options in front of him.

Mental ability tests that you might think of using include the AH series, devised by Alice Heim (hence the AH), the Thurstone Test of Mental Alertness, or the NIIP (National Institute of Industrial Psychology) Group Tests.

2. *Tests of specific aptitude or ability*

In many cases you will want to measure a candidate much more specifically than a general intelligence test allows. It is not so much a question of how bright is this candidate, or how quickly will she learn a new skill, but does she have the *specific* ability to do or learn what it is important to do or learn in this job? So you might want to know if the candidate has the aptitude to learn computer programming or a foreign language, for example.

Specific ability tests like these do exist. Among them are computer programming, mechanical ability (useful for engineering apprentices), manual dexterity (testing the ability to handle and place very small items, such as electronic components, with ease), clerical speed and accuracy, audio checking for secretaries and clerks, word processing aptitude, and many specific forms of verbal, numerical and spatial reasoning. I've listed some of these tests, along with their 'trade names' in Figure 8.2.

What makes us tick?

In my experience of testing applicants, I have found that employers are often more interested to know about applicants' personality than about their ability. They need answers to lots of

General Ability Tests
AH Series
Graduate and Managerial Assessment
SHL Advanced Test Battery
Thurstone Test of Mental Alertness
Watson Glaser Critical Thinking Appraisal

Specific Ability Tests
ACER Short Clerical Test
Speed and Accuracy Test
Mechanical Reasoning Test
Fine Dexterity Test
Ishihara Test of Colour Blindness
SHL Eosys Word Processing Aptitude Battery
SHL Programmer Aptitude Series

Personality Questionnaires
California Psychological Inventory
Gordon Personal Profile and Inventory
Myers–Briggs Type Indicator
Occupational Personality Questionnaire
Sixteen Personality Factor (16PF)

Note: These are just some of the reputable tests available. Whether they are suitable for the job in question depends very largely on the nature of the job.

Figure 8.2: Examples of Three Types of Psychological Tests

questions about the way the person typically behaves. What is she like as a person? Will she fit in? How will I get on with her? Does she have any traits which will get in the way of her performing? Is she too aggressive? Does she have a couldn't-care-less approach? These, and a thousand and one other personality characteristics, might make her less than perfect for you and your organization. It is these issues which you, as an employer, need to know before offering her the job.

So more and more recruiters are turning to personality questionnaires to help them get a better fix on a candidate than a short interview can do.

1. *Personality questionnaires*

I must stress at the outset that no personality questionnaire will give you answers to every question you might want to ask. They only give you answers that the applicant is prepared to tell you on a questionnaire. If a candidate doesn't want to reveal an alcohol problem, or an inability to get up in the morning, questionnaires are very unlikely to winkle the fact out. But they do give a broad view of what someone is like.

There are any number of personality tests on the market. Among the ones you may come across are the Occupational Personality Questionnaire (OPQ), the 16PF (standing for 16 Personality Factors), the Myers-Briggs Type Indicator, the Thomas International DISC test and the Gordon Personal Profile and Inventory.

I can recommend the Gordon Personal Profile, the OPQ, the Myers–Briggs and the 16PF, among others, when used properly.

The general format of these instruments is largely the same. There is a series of questions where you are asked to say whether you agree or disagree that the statement applies to you. Sometimes it is a Yes/No answer. More often you have a range or choice of answers, running from, say, 'very like me', through 'a little like me', to 'not at all like me'.

Here are two examples of personality questionnaires that you can try out on yourself. The first is part of a computerized Values Questionnaire which measures twenty-six different traits. This example looks at one trait, called Task Orientation. The full version is obtainable from Assessment Design Services Ltd (see Appendix).

The second questionnaire measures what is known as Type A behaviour.

BOX 2

Task Orientation Questionnaire

Instructions
For each of the 10 statements, choose one of the responses (a) to (e) which best applies to you.

(a) Disagree strongly
(b) Disagree
(c) Neutral
(d) Agree
(e) Strongly agree

Questionnaire

1. I enjoy delegating tasks to others.
2. The task is more important than people.
3. I am dependable and thorough.
4. I like working to deadlines.
5. Decisions are about getting the job done.
6. The job comes first – always.
7. Disagreements rarely interfere with getting the job done.
8. I never like the job to take second place.
9. You have to make sacrifices to get the task done.
10. I feel best when a job is finished.

When you have done it, score the answers as follows:

To score

(a) Disagree strongly = 0
(b) Disagree = 1
(c) Neutral = 2
(d) Agree = 3
(e) Strongly agree = 4

The higher the score the more task orientated you see yourself to be.

continued overleaf

People with **high task orientation** tend to be very concerned to get the job done; they are keen to get on with the task in hand. They often put getting the job done, and out of the way, before the people aspects of the job. They are not always the most sympathetic or sociable of people.

People with **low task orientation** tend to be the sort who play down the importance of the task. Instead, they are often more concerned with the needs of people. They may like to stop and chat, to hear about what people are saying, thinking and feeling. They are often keen to lend a sympathetic ear, listen to people's troubles and offer a kind thought or action. They tend to put the people concerns of a job before the task concerns. It's usually people first, task second.

BOX 3

Type A Personality Questionnaire

For each of the following ten statements, choose the one response which best applies to you.

1. I enjoy competition and winning:
   a) not much
   b) sometimes
   c) yes
2. I frequently check the time:
   a) no
   b) occasionally
   c) yes
3. I make up timetables for myself:
   a) rarely
   b) sometimes
   c) usually
4. I keep within the speed limit:
   a) usually
   b) sometimes
   c) rarely
5. I arrive on time for important engagements:
   a) rarely
   b) sometimes
   c) usually
6. I lose my temper under pressure:
   a) never
   b) sometimes
   c) often

continued overleaf

7. I am an ambitious person:
   a) no
   b) a little
   c) yes
8. I am often doing several things at once:
   a) no
   b) sometimes
   c) yes
9. I am a patient sort of person:
   a) yes
   b) sometimes
   c) no
10. I feel guilty when I am doing nothing:
    a) no
    b) sometimes
    c) yes

To score
a) = 0
b) = 1
c) = 2

Total

Below 7,	you are probably a Type B
7–10,	you are in the middle
10 plus,	you are probably a Type A
15 plus,	you are very much a Type A

Explanation

Type A people are achieving, competitive, impatient, aggressive, feel under time pressure, have a strong sense of duty and are often rather obsessional. They typically get very impatient with queues. Waiting for trains or in the Sainsbury checkout on a Saturday morning drives them bananas! Type As are apt to rush around, packing as much as possible into the available time. They cope rather poorly with stress. There is evidence that they are more prone to having heart attacks than the Type B. The good news is that Type A behaviour can be changed, if you want to.

Type B individuals are the opposite of the Type A. They tend to be laid back, easy going, unhurried and less competitive. They more easily roll with the punches. They are less obsessional, and take hiccups and problems with a more relaxed frame of mind. They don't always get as much done in the short term, but they

continued overleaf

may last longer. There is some research evidence that senior managers, surprisingly, are more often Type B than Type A. Perhaps it is because they cope with stress and strain, and are less prone to stress symptoms than their less fortunate Type A colleagues.

Note: These two personality questionnaires are abbreviated and adapted versions of longer, more authentic tests. They are not intended to be taken as authoritative views of your personality. Their purpose is to show you the kinds of questions, and the sort of characteristics, which can be measured by properly designed and validated personality questionnaires.

Do tests work?

Any measuring instrument, be it a thermometer, a tape measure, a car's speedometer, or a machine which speaks your weight, is only any use if it works. The same applies to psychological tests. If they measure accurately, we may be able to use them. If they discriminate between the good candidates and the poor, and don't discriminate unfairly on the grounds of race or gender, then there seems every reason to use them. But the $64,000 question is, do they in fact work?

First, we have to ask what we mean by the word 'work'. This is not just academic interest. If you decide to use tests, you have to know how to find out if they will work for you. There are loads of charlatans who will claim an instrument will help you select when it does no such thing. This part of the chapter should help you see through the slick sales pitch, and help you ask the right questions.

We need to get to grips with the meaning of two words – reliablity and validity.

Reliability refers to the consistency with which a test measures. If a doctor took your blood pressure today and then repeated it every day for the rest of the week, you wouldn't think much of this particular measure if it gave wildly different readings from day to day. So a measuring instrument must give *consistent* readings over time. On the other hand, when measuring people's blood pressure or weight, we wouldn't expect it to be totally consistent, even from one day to the next. We certainly wouldn't be altogether surprised if it gave a different result from one year to the next. After all, people just aren't that consistent or predictable. We may be upset one day, but not the next. We may put on weight one year and go on a diet another. But large swings in readings are unlikely unless we have had some major event in the period between.

The same is true for psychometric tests. Some aspects of our personality can change slowly as we get older. We may grow in confidence or become rather more quiet and controlled. But barring any major upheaval in our lives, our underlying personality (the core you) stays much as it always was. We would expect tests to reflect this stability in our behaviour.

So the first question to ask of any selection test is: is it reliable? The manual should contain reliability coefficients. This is a statistic which shows how close two readings from the instrument are over a period of time, i.e. how consistent the questionnaire is. Look for coefficients of +0.8 or above. If the manual doesn't report any, be suspicious and ask. If you get stalled by the sales person or test publisher, don't touch the test.

Validity is a little more involved. If refers to whether the test measures what it says it measures. Many so-called psychological questionnaires appear in magazines. They claim to tell you how good a lover you are, how caring you are, or how much fun you are to be with. They are amusing to do. People don't usually take them seriously, which is fortunate because they are unlikely to be valid.

The process of establishing the validity of a test is long and complicated. It involves comparing the results it gives with known differences between groups of people and with other tests measuring the same or similar concepts. Say a psychologist was designing a test to measure occupational stress. She would have to show that it distinguished between people who had signs or symptoms of stress, such as psychosomatic pains or rashes. And she would have to show that it gave similar results as lots of other tests designed to measure stress. All this takes time and money. It's not something you can do on the back of an envelope. This is the safeguard you need to look for if you are about to use a test to help pick a candidate. Look for evidence of the test's validity in the manual.

Let's take an example. Suppose you were proposing to use a test of general intellectual ability to select salespeople who would have to attend a rigorous product–knowledge training course before being sent out on the road to sell. You should look in the manual to see what validity information it contains. This may show that it has been used on college students. Look to see if those who did better, by getting more exam passes for example, also did better on the test. After all, if it is supposed to measure intellectual ability, or the ability to learn, it should distinguish between those who are bright and those who are not so bright, as measured by exam passes.

Again, the same caution should grip you if it contains no validity data. Ask for it. If the answers you get are not convincing, leave the test alone and choose another that is better supported with evidence. Don't be swayed by recommendations that well known companies are using it. I know of at least one test that is used extensively by major 'blue chip' British companies. Yet validity studies show that it is virtually worthless. Remember, buyer beware. The tests I've already talked about are reliable and valid when properly used.

How can I get hold of tests?

If you decide testing of candidates seems like a good idea, how do you go about putting in a testing programme?

Reputable tests can only be obtained through a limited number of suppliers. Names and addresses can be found in the Appendix to this book. These suppliers will insist that you go through a training course to learn how to administer, score and interpret the test before they will let you buy supplies. A cynic may say that this is restrictive practice and good for the test publishers but not for the end user. In truth, there is more to it than that. Tests are delicate instruments. They can be used for the wrong purpose, wrongly administered, poorly interpreted, and the security and confidentiality of the instrument and the result can be ignored. This is not fair on candidates or responsible test users. So the test publisher wants to be sure that they will be used in a professional way and the training programme is designed to ensure that they are. In essence there are four major ways in which you can install a selection testing procedure. They are:

- Get yourself trained
- Use a consultant
- Use your own staff
- Use a computer

1. *Getting yourself trained up*
There are a number of approved training courses for the use of psychological tests. They usually last somewhere between two days and a week per test, but an introductory course on the principles of psychological testing may be a pre-requisite. They last around a week. A list of approved courses can be obtained from the British Psychological Society (BPS) and the Institute of Personnel Management (IPM). Addresses can be found at the back of the book.

There are a number of advantages to getting yourself trained. These are:

- *Advantages*

a) Once you have undergone the training, you are free to use the test as often as you like. If you are doing a lot of testing, this can be a big saving over using consultants.

b) You will understand the benefits and limitations of using tests. Assuming you think they are a good idea, you can more easily convince sceptics, both colleagues and candidates.

c) You can learn how to build up your own comparison data (called norms) to compare with a particular candidate's score.

But the advantages can easily be outweighed by the disadvantages. These are:

- *Disadvantages*

a) Each course is only for one test and there are thousands of tests on the market. While you are unlikely to want to use more than half a dozen or so, you will want to use more than one if you are going to do the job properly. Six courses cost a lot of money.

b) It is not just the cost of the fees for attending the course. There are the costs of travelling, accommodation and of being away from work.

c) You may have to take advice on which tests to use for a particular job and so which training course to go on.

d) All test publishers charge for the question booklets, answer sheets and scoring keys, which you will have to keep buying. Some charge a licence fee which has to be renewed each year. This really makes the cost mount up.

2. *Independent consultants*
A better alternative is often to employ an outside consultant. They should be chartered psychologists, preferably occupational psychologists. Contact the BPS for a list of these.

Such a person should make it their business to find out about the job, probably by a systematic job analysis (see Chapter 2). They will then be able to advise on the most relevant battery of tests, administer them, feed back the results to the candidate, and write a report for the client company on the results of the testing programme.

- *Advantages*

a) Where you have a relatively small number of candidates, say less than fifteen to twenty a year, this is often your most cost effective way of testing candidates.

b) A good consultant should have at her disposal a range of test instruments, far more than you alone would wish to be trained for, and be able to choose the most appropriate.

c) She is likely to be more skilled than you at administering and interpreting the results. Just as important, she will have had a lot of experience at feeding results back to applicants who have been tested. This is good practice, since it makes it more likely that a candidate will look on the testing in a positive light and will know where she has done well or not so well. But it is not always an easy job to tell a candidate to her face that she is below the required standard on an ability test, say. Better to let the consultant do the dirty work!

• *Disadvantages*

a) As you might expect, the biggest is the cost. Consultants don't come cheap.

b) Finding someone suitable can be a problem. Ring the BPS. Or ask someone you trust who has used a consultant occupational psychologist for a recommendation.

3. *Employing your own full-time staff*

Some large organizations, such as the Civil Service, the Post Office, British Telecom, Shell and British Airways have specialist departments employing occupational psychologists. Engaging full-time professional testing staff is only really an option for large employers.

4. *Computerized testing*

A useful new development is automated testing. You can buy tests that can be administered, scored and interpreted on a microcomputer. It's like having an expert on a disc. Again, names and addresses of suppliers are given at the end of the book.

• *Advantages*

a) It is always available. Your consultant-on-a-disc is never away on business or on holiday just when you need them.

b) It's easy. Just explain the purpose of the testing session to the candidate, load the disc into the computer and sit the candidate in front of the screen. The computer takes care of the rest. It will even print out the results either for you, for the candidate, or for both.

• *Disadvantages*

a) Cost. The discs involve many person-hours of work to devise and program. This has to be reflected in the cost. Many discs have a certain number of administrations, fifty say, before you have to buy another disc. Or there are hefty annual licensing fees.

b) You may still be expected to go on a short training course to learn to interpret the results that the computer prints out.

c) Without advice you may have problems deciding which test to buy for which job. One way round this is that some discs now come with as many as fifteen tests per disc. But do you really want your candidate sitting doing test for five hours or so?

Key points

1. Tests are useful aids to making better selection decisions.

2. There are three categories of tests commonly used in selection. These are:

    - General mental ability
    - Specific aptitudes and ability
    - Personality

3. Mental ability tests measure how well someone is able to reason in an abstract way, and relate to the ability to learn a new skill. For this reason, they are commonly used for apprentice and management trainee selection.

4. Specific aptitude and ability tests measure particular skills such as computer programming, clerical speed and manual dexterity, among a host of others.

5. Personality tests measure self-reported typical behaviour and are popular for jobs with lots of people contact.

6. You need to be sure that the tests you use are reliable and valid if they are going to be of any use in selection.

7. Access to tests is limited to those with knowledge on how to use and interpret them. You can:

    - Get yourself trained
    - Use a consultant
    - Employ your own trained staff
    - Use a computer (a test on a disc)

9 Tests to Avoid

'The most costly of all follies is to believe passionately in the palpably not true.'

H. L. Mencken

'Sometimes I've believed as many as six impossible things before breakfast.'

Lewis Carroll

There are so many tests on the market, and so many people wanting to sell you the tests and the expensive training programme that goes with them, that it is very difficult to decide on which are good tests and which are useless. So how do you choose a good test?

The first answer to this is that no test is going to be good for you if you haven't decided what you want to measure with the test. So you should have gone through the steps outlined in earlier chapters concerning job analysis and personnel specifications.

Then look at the test you propose to use.

What Makes a Good Test?

Before any reputable test is put on sale to registered users it should be designed to certain standards and undergo trials.

For a *personality, personal values or interest questionnaire* the designer will:

1. Decide on the traits the test will measure, based on a theory of human behaviour or a statistical analysis. Usually both.

2. Choose questions for the test according to how well they distinguish between people who are known to be high or low on the chosen traits.

3. Standardize the questionnaire. This involves getting a large cross-section of the population to complete it. Then statements about a particular individual's personality are based on factual comparisons with other people, not on a hunch that they seem different or similar.

For *mental ability* tests (intelligence tests, for example) the steps are similar:

1. All the questions in the test should be tested on a large number of people. This is to make sure that they are clear and unambiguous in their meaning and that they are neither too easy nor too difficult.

2. The questions that remain are statistically tested to see whether they are measuring one thing, say verbal reasoning ability, or a number of factors. Inappropriate ones are discarded.

3. Standardization. Trials take place to see how many people score in a range. For a test with fifty questions, we need to know how many get them all right. How many get forty-nine out of fifty, how many forty-eight, and so on. A person's score on its own is pretty meaningless unless we can compare it with a group of similar people. Standardization groups should be large if they are to give meaningful comparisons. Three or four hundred is the absolute minimum. Usually the scores of many thousands of people are included in the test's manual.

Without these necessary steps, the test is no more use for selecting people than a list of general knowledge questions made up for a Christmas quiz.

How to Spot a Suspect Test

Investigate the manual

Look in the manual to see if the test you are being asked to buy has gone through the all-important vetting process outlined above.

Look for reliability and validity evidence

Another clue to look for is the reliability and validity evidence I talked about in the previous chapter. On the question of reliability, does the manual give reliability coefficients? Are these coefficients above about +0.8 for ability tests and +0.6 for personality questionnaires? For validity, does it give statistics (called norm tables) for how typical groups of employees differ on the test? Do these differences look sensible? If you have to answer 'No' to any of these questions, then be very wary. You probably have a duff test on your hands.

Short is suspect

Length alone is no guarantee of worth. But a test that is very short (say twenty questions or less) should raise your suspicions. Just think about it. There is no magic to tests. They just ask a series of questions about you, and then feed back the results to you or the tester using a particular framework of ideas. So how can a test be very accurate if it just asks a few questions? You cannot expect to find out anything very profound about someone if you ask less than twenty simple questions, can you? Phony or pseudo tests are typically very short, with just a couple of dozen items. You should be doubly sceptical if it claims to measure more than one characteristic, yet needs only twenty or so answers.

No-hopers of the Testing World

Graphology

Graphology (or handwriting analysis) seems so easy, cheap and so obviously interpretable that it just must tell us something about people, mustn't it? Unfortunately not. This is probably because the way we write depends on how we were taught, or the hurry we are in when writing, rather than reflecting personality traits.

There have been a number of scientific studies to see whether graphology does measure personality, and they have come to much the same conclusion. It is of little value to use it as a measure of personality, or anything else that might be useful to help the selection of people for jobs. I'll give you just two examples from this mass of research. One study gave handwriting samples from estate agents to graphologists. Their ratings of the estate agents were completely unrelated to sales figures or the ratings of supervisors who knew them. Another study of insurance salesmen was equally unsuccessful in predicting success.

There is only one piece of evidence that it does measure any psychological trait and that is that it can indicate gross abnormalities of the personality. This is the sort of psychological handicap that anyone would be likely to spot in anyone else, whether they saw their handwriting or not. It does not tell us how extrovert, sociable, easy-going, assertive a person is, or anything about the kind of qualities or characteristics that we need to know before employing someone.

Other evidence shows that graphologists cannot agree among themselves about assessments from the same handwriting.

Despite this, graphology is regularly used on the continent of Europe. A recent study by a student of mine showed that, although it was extremely rarely used in Britain, around half the major companies in France used it to help select employees. So don't be fooled. Just because a method is used doesn't mean that it's valid.

Lie detectors and 'honesty' tests

It is very important in many jobs that the employee is honest. These jobs include bank employees, shop assistants, government communication workers, spies and anyone who has access to cash or merchandise as part of their job. So it is natural that people have searched for methods that have a good probability of spotting the less honest and weeding them out before they are offered a job.

One approach to this has been the 'lie detector' or polygraph as it is more technically known. We have all experienced the chill, wet, clammy, 'cold sweat' feeling on our skin and the increase in breathing rate, when we are anxious or afraid. The design of the polygraph is based on this experience. It works by detecting minute changes in electrical resistance on the skin and other body changes caused by changes in moisture of the skin. Supposedly, when we are connected up to the machine and questioned, the polygraph will detect when we are telling lies by spotting these changes.

The problem is the number of times it detects lying in honest people who are scared of the test, and the number of times it misses the genuine criminal either because he doesn't see what he is doing as dishonest or because he doesn't react.

Using the polygraph for selection is banned in many states in the USA. But it is legal in Britain, even though the British Psychological Society has published the research evidence showing it to be suspect, and many trade unionists oppose it.

Paper and pencil forms of honesty testing are also available, but the few that I've seen don't convince me on reliability and validity grounds.

A better method for trying to spot those who are dishonest at work is to use references (see Chapter 7), though this, too, is a hit and miss affair.

Palmistry

It's amazing how many different ways there are that – at least someone will claim – tell us about ourselves. Reading the palm of your hand is one. You might have thought that such an arcane art had been banished to the history books. No, it is alive and well. Only this year a book was published claiming to be able to tell you how to spot business acumen by thumb size, shape of palm, length of fingers, and the amount you squeeze someone's hand in a handshake.

As a rule of thumb (you might say), the two crucial fingers for business purposes are the index and the little finger. To add to the mystique, these are called Jupiter and Mercury.

Jupiter is supposed to be the sign of leadership, status and magnetism (the personal charisma sort, not the school experiments with iron fillings variety). Watch out for bosses with a long Jupiter. They are autocratic, cruel, arrogant and intolerant.

If your Mercury is 'reasonably' long, it means you have ambition, achievement, drive and leadership (again). An overlong Mercury is a sign of deceitfulness.

Square-handed people with small fingers work best alone. So don't take a square hand as your right-hand man or woman. The best shape to have if you want to make money is the large hand with thick fingers widening slightly at the tips, and a hard unyielding palm. These are the signs of the budding millionaire, we are told.

Now you can take a rest to study your own palm, and catch us up later.

To the best of my knowledge, there is not a scrap of evidence to show that palmistry tells us anything about our personalities. But I expect you knew that all along.

Why do Some Methods Seem to Work, Which Don't?

I have been very negative about the methods above. The basis of my criticisms is the result of scientifically controlled experiments and carefully designed surveys. So, if I am right (and I am!) that these procedures have nothing useful to contribute to professional and systematic selection, why is it, you may ask, that so many of the methods *seem* so plausible? Descriptions of us produced by these methods often sound so right. The personality blurb produced by the sales person who has just tested us seems impressively accurate. But then, horoscopes often ring true and fortune tellers can be very convincing. So where's the catch?

The answer lies in the nature of the language used to describe us. If it is general enough, with sufficient 'weasel words' and vagueness, it will convince most of us. Take the passage below, typical of many predictions made by astrologists in the popular daily papers.

> Money will concern you in the next few weeks. You may soon have an unpleasant meeting with a colleague or friend, but they mean no harm. Try to look on the bright side if depressed.

If we take the short passage apart, you can easily see that it can apply to the vast majority of people.

Most of us are concerned with money at one time or another, and for many it is a constant worry. Even those with wealth have to concern themselves with holding on to it or investing it wisely. As for the second sentence, unpleasantness between people is a common occurrence, even those we love or consider as our friends. Whether others mean harm is very difficult to say. The home-spun philosophy in the final sentence is also very easy to agree with as a general prescription for dealing with minor upsets, even if it tells us very little of a practical nature.

The point is that tests need to be *precise*. Without precise information you can't choose between candidates. You can't separate one from another.

Key points

1. Proper tests have to go through a lengthy design process. This includes:
    - Statistical analysis of the test questions to check that they mean the same thing to different people, and hang together as one factor
    - Standardization, to be able to compare one person with another
2. Spotting a genuine test is not easy. Pointers you can look for are:

- A comprehensive manual showing the design steps
- Validity and reliability data
- Data on different groups of people (called norms)
- More than a dozen or so items, particularly if the test claims to measure more than one personality trait

3. Tests with little to recommend them include:

   - Graphology (handwriting analysis)
   - Lie detectors
   - Palmistry

4. Just because the personality description produced by a test sounds accurate, doesn't mean that it is useful. Descriptions can be written which may be true, in a woolly sort of way, but which don't separate one candidate from another.

10 Other Selection Methods

> 'As I grow older, I pay less attention to what men say, I just watch what they do.'
>
> *Andrew Carnegie*

Work Samples

What are they?

Work sample tests are just as the name suggests. They are tests that sample the work.

Applicants for jobs involving typing are commonly given a typing test. You have probably given one out yourself. This is a good example of a work sample test. It samples the work the successful candidate will have to do, or at least part of it.

Often, though, secretarial candidates are given any old document that happens to be lying around and asked to type it. This is a poor work sample. It is unstandardized (i.e. one person's score can't be compared with another's) subjectively scored, and tells you little about how good an all-round secretary the person will be, which is usually what you want to know. Even if you restrict it to testing how good a copy typist someone is, you need to standardize the test and objectively score it. But, limited as it is, this sort of typing test is better than nothing. Certainly, it is better than the leading interview question of 'you're a good typist, I suppose?' (see Chapter 6 for more examples of leading questions.)

A better idea is to get hold of some relatively cheap, commercially available secretarial and clerical work sample tests which are standardized. They are available from the test suppliers given in the Appendix.

The most common types of work sample test are the so-called psychomotor. This just means using your hands. Apart from typing, there are using tools, assembling items, sewing, wiring, and so on. For the job of maintenance mechanic, for example, you might have to install a starter motor, wire up a bulb so that it lights up, or repair a gearbox.

How do they work?

If you want to know how to select a good teacher, follow a good teacher around, watch what she does and make a list of these activities. Then get hopeful teachers to do a few of these tasks while you watch and keep score. The same goes for policemen, train drivers, lumberjacks, and just about any job you can think of. Mind you, it's not all that easy to devise realistic samples of jobs. Think of an astronaut if you want a difficult one.

The main difference between work sample testing and psychometric testing is the realism of the test. Paper and pencil tests are really signs that the candidate has the required ability or personality to do the job. They are not direct measures. We have to interpret the test result and infer how good a candidate will be. A woman scores highly on an intelligence test, so we assume she is bright, which in turn makes us assume she will be a good research chemist. The fact is that psychologists can show good evidence why intelligence is correlated with performance in lots of jobs, but it is still an assumption.

Work samples are much more direct. They tap the particular skill required in the job in a much more straightforward way.

Careful preparation is needed, however. Job analysis and other background work has to go in to make sure that the work sample is a valid indicator of performance in a particular job. The example I gave earlier of following around a job holder is often a major part of job analysis. Just because a work sample seems relevant dosen't mean that it is. Look for evidence that its design was based on relevant job analysis.

Why use work samples?

There are a number of advantages to the work sample test. One important one is that it often gives the candidate a good idea of what the job will be like (a 'realistic job preview', see Chapter 3). An applicant may find that she doesn't like the job when she has done a small part of it. It's much better for all concerned that she withdraws now rather than after she has taken it on. In a work sample test for the job of sewer mechanic in Miami Beach, not surprisingly, quite a few applicants withdrew after a test sample of life in an underground sewer.

The second has already been mentioned. Applicants often prefer work sample tests to paper and pencil ones because they see them as a fairer method of testing their ability. They have what psychologist call 'face validity'. This means that they *seem* on the face of it to measure relevant skills. Face validity counts for a lot if you want candidates to accept testing.

Using work samples for spotting who will succeed at training

One problem with psychomotor (manual) work samples is that they can only be used to choose between candidates who already know the job. After all, they give someone a taste of the job itself and look to see how they get on. If you've never done the job before, you won't do very well. There is no point asking someone to translate a passage from Finnish to English if they can't tell Finnish from Serbo-Croat.

This is no real problem in most cases; usually you want to select from among applicants who are experienced. But in some cases this is not so. Selecting trainees or apprentices is an obvious example. They know little or nothing about the job, yet. What you, the selector, wants to find out is: can they *learn* to do the job if they are given training?

This is where we come to something called trainability tests, a form of work sample. They aim to tell whether someone can learn the skills needed in the job. What happens is this. An instructor gives directions and a demonstration, sometimes gives chance for a practice, then gets the candidate to have a go. The instructor rates the performance of the candidate using a checklist or rating scale. A checklist for bricklaying might have items like:

Did/didn't use the correct sand/cement mix
Did/didn't use enough water in the mix
Did/didn't lay bricks evenly
Did/Didn't use enough mortar
Did/Didn't use spacers

Candidates can judge their own peformance on these tests. This has the benefit I referred to earlier. They may decide that the job isn't for them if they find learning the sample a struggle. Result – you and the candidate are saved from wasted training.

How to design work samples

Using work samples assumes that they are truly similar to the real training programme or the job in question. The kind of steps that you have to go through to devise a typical work sample are:

1. Draw up a list of all the key tasks. These are the activities that have to be done frequently and are important in doing the job well. People who are expert at the job should do this.

2. Decide what separates the effective from the ineffective peformer in terms of what they do on the job.

3. Consider what is the level of skill typical applicants have already. This is to try and make the work samples neither too easy nor too difficult. If they are too easy, everyone will succeed. If too difficult, no one will succeed. Either way, the test won't discriminate between candidates. The help of a personnel expert familiar with recruitment and selection is useful here.

4. Then you are in a position to decide which tasks the sample should include. These should be common to all of the first three steps. That way you hope that the work sample is representative of the skills of the job and the skills already possessed.

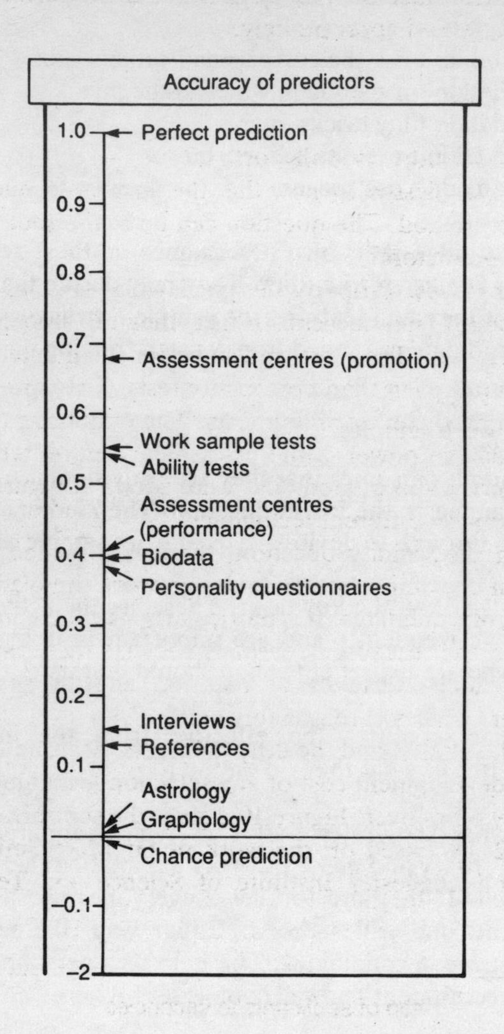

Figure 10.1 *Source:* Adapted from work by Mike Smith, published in *Personnel Management* (December 1986).

5. Draw up rating scales and checklists to score a candidate's performance. Consider all the ways it could be performed and score the best method appropriately.

Is it all worth it?

It sounds a lot of effort. Is it all worth it?

You may have guessed by now that the answer depends on the validity of the method. The question can be rephrased: are work samples valid predictors?

The answer is yes. Properly designed work samples are very good predictors of later success. In fact, they are among the best methods there are. They are much better than interviews or references. Better even than personality tests. They are generally just as valid a predictor as ability tests. The only thing that beats them for predictive power is the assessment centre, which is an expensive combination of methods. Take a look at Figure 10.1 for a comparison of the different techniques.

Apart from the validity question, there is a second factor to consider when deciding whether to design work sample test. This is the number of candidates. It is particularly worth the investment if you will use the test often (perhaps because there are regular vacancies or annual intakes of recruits) and the number of candidates per vacancy is reasonably high.

With good validity and healthy numbers of candidates per vacancy, the development cost of any selection technique can pay for itself many times over. Figure 10.2 gives the sums. Both Figure 10.1 and 10.2 are based on the work of Dr Mike Smith at the University of Manchester Institute of Science and Technology (UMIST).

	Ratio of applicants to vacancies		
Validity coefficient	3:1	6:1	10:1
0.1	39	45	61
0.2	77	91	122

0.3	116	137	183
0.4	154	182	245
0.5	192	228	306
0.6	231	273	368
0.7	270	368	429

You can see that very large gains can be made. You get the best return on investment by using a method that has high validity (such as work samples) with a large number of candidates per vacancy.

Example

Say you're recruiting sales people who get paid £15,000 a year. You know from experience that, on average, sales reps stay with you about 3 years and you have 6 serious applicants for each vacancy. Work samples have validities around 0.5. Using figure 2 you can see that this method would give you a saving of £228 for each £1,000 of salary. So the sums work out as:

£228 × 15 × 3 years = £10,260.

Take away the cost of designing the work sample, say £5,000, and you are still left with a saving of £5,260.

The next occasion saves you another £10,260. If you appoint 7 representatives a year, the sums make the investment really worthwhile. They are:

£10,260 × 7 appointments = 71,820
£71,820 – £5,000 development costs = £66,820

Terms and assumptions

The term validity coefficient you came across in Chapter 6. It is a scale of how efficiently a measure, such as the interview, predicts success at the job.

The figures in the table are based on some very complex statistical assumptions. One of the more important ones is the standard deviation or worker performance. This statistic represents the difference in work performance between the good and not-so-good employees. It assumes that this standard deviation is about one third of the wage paid.

Figure 10.2: Savings per £1,000 Salary

Do I have to go through that lengthy design process?

The design sounds long and complicated. You may be wondering if it is necessary to do all that to get the benefits.

The answer is that it is the only sure way of getting the results you need from the method. Any short cuts in the design mean that you risk losing the benefits. I've said that it is very cost effective if you have a lot of people to select. But what if you don't?

My own view is that, in cases like this, you can devise your own work sample without the elaborate preparation. This is heresy to the purist. But you won't go far wrong if you:

1. Know the job well.

2. Consider what it is that the job requires to be done, especially the tasks that really make the difference.

3. Standardize the conditions, so that every candidate gets the same work sample under the same conditions.

4. Have an agreed list of performance criteria so that eveyone uses the same ones to judge by.

5. Measure the performance using judges who know the job, with more than one assessor present.

This is certainly better than relying on asking someone about how they would tackle the job.

An example

Let's take an example. A management college I know uses informal work samples as part of the selection prodedure for tutors. What really matters in this job is being able to get across ideas to managers.

The college asks shortlisted candidates to take a session, lasting anywhere between one hour and half a day, on a real course that is taking place in the college. Experienced college tutors are in the audience and compare notes afterwards.

Candidates know about the test many days beforehand, so they have time to prepare. Most have held similar posts at training colleges before and know what to expect of their audience. It may be nerve racking for the candidate, having fellow professionals in the audience, but it mirrors very well what they will have to do week in, week out, to earn their daily crust.

In-Tray Exercises

In-tray exercises are simulations of a manager's job and are a kind of work sample. Their purpose is to capture many of the tasks performed by a manager and test the candidate on the skills required to deal with these tasks.

To picture an in-tray exercise, imagine you have been away from work for a week or two. You come into the office early on your first day back. There in front of you in your in-tray is a pile of papers. There are memos, messages of telephone calls, monthly reports, hand-written notes, letters from clients and suppliers, salary data, minutes of meetings, and so on. It's a typical bad day at the office. What you have to do is make decisions based on the information in front of you. You may have to allocate priorities, decide what you'll do yourself and what you'll delegate, decide on what action to take, etc. All you have is a pad of paper and maybe a telephone. There is no one around to consult as nobody but you is yet in the office. You have limited time, usually an hour or an hour and a half. That, in essence, is an in-tray exercise.

They are being used more and more for executive selection, often in combination with other methods such as tests and interviews.

The specific abilities assessed by the in-tray exercise depend on the job and the design of the particular exercise. Typical skills are:

Reading and understanding
Problem analysis
Problem solving

Written communication skills
Judgement
Decision making
Establishing priorities
Planning and organizing
Delegation
Supervision of others

At their simplest, in-trays boil down to two measures:

1. Planning or administration (an intellectual or problem solving ability).
2. Supervision or delegation (a human relations skill).

It is far preferable to have the exercise designed specifically for the job, so that it simulates the real thing as closely as possible. However, if a particular job is on offer only a limited number of times, which will mostly be the case in executive appointments, this is not a realistic option. Then, off-the-shelf in-tray exercises can be used with suitable training. A list of suppliers is given in the Appendix.

Scoring the results should be done by trained assessors who are knowledgeable about the job. It is important to have the scoring as objective as possible, with responses categorized as good, or not so good, based on samples of previous employees who have done the exercise.

Test yourself

Now you can have a go at an in-tray exercise for yourself. It is loosely based on one myself and a colleague wrote for a computer company. It was used as part of the selection procedure for sales people. While I don't expect you to perform like an experienced computer sales person, it does at least show you what such exercises are all about.

Turn to the next chapter and have a go.

When you've done it, have a look at the Answers page (p. 171). This gives you guidelines on how to score your answers.

Key points

1. Work sample tests take small, representative pieces of the job and use them to test candidates.

2. They give a candidate a chance to try out the work to see if they like it.

3. You can use a particular form of work sample, known as trainability tests, to predict who will succeed at training.

4. Work samples have a good record of predicting later job performance.

5. They are costly to design and generally need to be tailor-made. But they are very cost effective if used with large numbers of candidates.

6. In-tray exercises are a form of work sample. They simulate parts of a manager's job. The skills they measure include:

   - Reading and understanding
   - Problem analysis
   - Problem solving
   - Written communication skills
   - Judgement
   - Decision making
   - Establishing priorities
   - Planning and organizing
   - Delegation
   - Supervision of others

11 Sales In-tray Exercise

'The best effect of any book is that it excites the reader to self activity.' *Thomas Carlyle*

Background

An important element in any sales job is the ability to organize and plan one's workload. In order to do this, a sales person must be able to prioritize, resolve conflicts of priority, and respond flexibly to any unexpected demands or changes in his or her workload.

The following exercise provides a structured way of gathering information about how this is achieved by you.

Task

This exercise requires you to schedule a number of tasks for the coming week.

For the purposes of this exercise, the time is 9.30 am on the first Monday of the month. You are in your office in the centre of Midtown and you have forty-five minutes before you have to leave the office for a meeting which will last until 2.00 pm that day. During this time you must plan your work for the coming week in order to deal with a list of tasks and events (shown on p. 165).

Although the circumstances are hypothetical, you should treat the exercise as realistically as possible. Build into your timetable all the other tasks (such as administration, travelling time, etc) which you will have to do to complete the workload. Where an item does not specify a particular day or time for its completion, you may assume that others will be able to fit in with you. You have no administrative back-up other than the shared use of a copy typist in the same building.

You have the use of a company car. No town or firm is further than ten miles away.

First, decide what is fundamental This is the most important task you would be sure to do, and any over-riding issues that you would take into account.

Then, schedule the thirteen items and write these in on the attached timetable. Include any administration time which you consider necessary. Write on the item questionnaire the factors you took into account in deciding when and how you would deal with each item. You can indicate on the questionnaire if you chose to carry some items over to the following week. If you need further information on any item before being able to deal with it, say so on the questionnaire.

Complete the questionnaire in note form. You may find it helpful to write this up as you go through the exercise, rather than filling it in at the end.

Summary

You have forty-five minutes to:

- decide on any fundamental points
- schedule thirteen items into your timetable
- complete the item questionnaire explaining the factors you took into account

Materials

1. List of thirteen tasks and events to be scheduled.
2. One week's timetable (one sheet).
3. Questionnaire (four sheets).

Tasks and Events to be Scheduled

1. Cyril Leith of ABC Company has left a telephone message. He is a potentially important customer based in Readyville whom you have been trying to arrange a meeting with for some time. He agrees to your invitation and would be able to see you for lunch on Wednesday if that suits you. No location was specified.

2. You have identified twenty-five potential customers whom you plan to speculatively phone (cold call) during the coming week.

3. You have been invited to attend a two-day national trade fair at a local Exhibition Centre on Tuesday and Wednesday this week. You know that a number of your existing customers, as well as other potential clients, will be attending for some of the time.

4. You have already arranged to see Susan Chappell, Managing Director of a large company in Willington on Thursday morning. You hope to close the sale that day.

5. Midcare Plc (based in Midtown) are long-standing and valuable customers. They phoned the previous Friday while you were out to say that they have found a new supplier who has more competitive rates than your company. They were grumbling about your prices. Your records tell you that Midcare were due to re-order within the next two to three weeks.

6. Tanya Jones, an old friend who lives locally, is setting up a new company. She is aiming for a specialist, up-market clientele, and is interested in using quality products from a reputable company like yours. She is eager to see you this week to get your advice and guidance.

7. The regular Round Table lunch is scheduled for Friday. You have found these useful in the past for meeting new contacts and getting information about potential customers. The lunch takes

place in the centre of Midtown at 12.30 until (usually) mid-afternoon.

8. Bob Weakes of Fiasco Ltd in Ableville is due a customer courtesy call. He is a regular customer and has not been seen for three weeks. It's about time for him to place an order.

9. There has been a telephone call from a customer while you were out. The message was that he is dissatisfied about some aspect of your company's service. It sounds like another delivery mess-up. He wishes to see you in relation to this matter. This is the third such complaint in the last few weeks.

10. Bumblewood Ltd are potential customers whom you saw last week. They are interested in doing business with you but left a message to say that on consideration of the quantity of business they can put your way, they want to negotiate a more favourable price. The would prefer to meet face-to-face on Thursday.

11. The Sales Manager of Modes Plc, a prospective customer based five miles away, has suggested that you call in to see him on Thursday. You have been trying to arrange a meeting for some weeks now, and he has been very difficult to contact.

12. Ken Woolley of Midtown, who has done a small amount of business with your company on a trial basis, is due to decide whether to use you exclusively and abandon his previous company. You suspect that if he is wavering now, he won't be convinced over the telephone. You have managed to find out from his secretary that he is in the office and relatively free all day on Tuesday.

13. You have been planning a golf day for three existing clients. All have been asked to keep their diaries free for Tuesday, and you are due to confirm with them today.

TIMETABLE							
	Monday	Tuesday	Wednesday	Thursday	Friday	Saturday	Sunday
08.00							
09.00							
10.00							
11.00							
12.00							
13.00							
14.00							
15.00							
16.00							
17.00							
18.00							
19.00							
20.00							

ITEM QUESTIONNAIRE AND TYPICAL ANSWERS

ITEM: 1

Factors taken into account when planning:

He is a busy man. He has set aside time to see me. I will organise it for Wednesday lunch.

Additional information required, if any:

ITEM: 2

Factors taken into account when planning:

Can be fitted in where necessary. Not on Friday afternoon – bad time for this type of canvassing.

Additional information required, if any:

ITEM: 3

Factors taken into account when planning:

Good base for future enquiries. One day is long enough. Also hectic schedule so 2 days would be impractical. Can't cancel

Additional information required, if any: golf.

ITEM: 4

Factors taken into account when planning:

A pre-arranged meeting must not be broken.

Additional information required, if any:

ITEM: 5

Factors taken into account when planning:

Valuable customers and must be contacted immediately. Go and see them today if possible.

Additional information required, if any:

ITEM: 6

Factors taken into account when planning:

Although there is no business here, potentially this friend could be a valuable contact. I would see her socially over dinner.

Additional information required, if any:

ITEM: 7

Factors taken into account when planning:

As nothing else needs urgent attention on Friday lunchtime, this would be foolish to miss.

Additional information required, if any:

ITEM: 8

Factors taken into account when planning:

Important to keep contact with regular customers. Must call in. Fit it in when I have a day of calls.

Additional information required, if any:

ITEM: 9
Factors taken into account when planning:

Needs URGENT attention before other things. Try and sort out today.

Additional information required, if any:

ITEM: 10
Factors taken into account when planning:

They must be seen on Thursday.

Additional information required, if any:

ITEM: 11
Factors taken into account when planning:

This fits in to Thursday's schedule, etc.

Additional information required, if any:

ITEM: 12
Factors taken into account when planning:

Although a smallish customer, I will see him Tuesday. I'll make it early because of golf.

Additional information required, if any:

ITEM: 13
Factors taken into account when planning:
As 3 people have kept a day free, for something I initiated. I must also be free, and not let them down.
Additional information required, if any:

Your Answers

Sales people in different jobs have different priorities. So the answers below can't be taken as gospel. Each company ought to design a different exercise for their validity study checks to see whether successful sales people in the job do the exercise differently from the less successful.

What follows is the sort of analysis that results. This is loosely based on an in-tray exercise I constructed and validated for a computer company. So where it refers to 'successful sales people' it really means 'successful sales people in this computer company'. But it gives you the idea. See how well you did.

Fundamental points

1. The delivery difficulty is the most important and urgent task.
2. The existing arrangements with customers must be honoured.

Successful sales people	*Less successful sales people*
Are prepared to ignore the trade fair (item 3)	Spend half a day or more at the trade fair
Spread speculative phone calls (cold calls) during the week (item 2)	Bunch cold calls together
Never put cold calls on a Friday, especially afternoons	Put cold calls on Fridays

Spend almost a whole day on golf with three valued customers (item 13)	Shorten the golf day to fit other major things in
Valued customer complaining about price dealt with by an immediate phone call (item 5)	Importance and urgency of grumbling customer issue less recognized
Realistic about timing. Never dealt with more than four items in one day	Over-committed themselves by putting five items or more in one day
Used phone often	Used letters often
Friend given low priority (e.g. for a drink in the evening) (item 6)	Friend seen during the day

Scoring

If you got at least one of the fundamental points, plus four or more of the items on the 'successful' side on the list, you did well.

12 Discriminating Fairly

> 'Prejudice is the reason of fools.'
>
> *Voltaire*

> 'I have a dream . . . that my four little children will one day live in a nation where they will not be judged by the colour of their skin but by the content of their character.'
>
> *Martin Luther King*

Selecting is all about discriminating. It is about you or me choosing one person in preference to another.

Assessment for selection is about trying to predict the future. It's about crystal-ball gazing. As selectors, we try to discriminate according to whether we think a person will do the job well in the future, if appointed.

Yet there is no law in Britain to stop someone discriminating against someone because of their sexual orientation or age. You may think, as I do, that to discriminate in this way is unfair, unethical and blinkered. Unlike in the USA, though, it is not illegal in this country. As a selector you have a lot of power.

What is against the law is to contravene the 1975 Sex Discrimination Act or the 1976 Race Relations Act. If you do, you could find yourself in court. These Acts apply not only to recruitment and selection but also to the promotion and transfer of all staff. The number of referrals to tribunals and to the courts of sex and race discrimination cases has increased in recent years. The way things are going, if you, as an employer, discriminate illegally you can expect to be given an increasingly rough ride in the courts.

So what must you do or not do so as to discriminate fairly? That is what this chapter aims to tell you.

General Principles

The Acts are designed to help eliminate discrimination in employment on the grounds of race and sex. They are very similar in their approach and have many provisions in common. In the areas of recruitment and initial appointment they prohibit discrimination:

1. In the arrangements made to decide who will be offered employment (such as different questions asked of a candidate based on race or sex).

2. In the employment terms offered to that person (such as different rates of pay or conditions of work).

3. By refusing or deliberately omitting to offer that person employment (such as deliberately leaving a person off a shortlist because of his or her race or sex).

It is also unlawful to discriminate against an *existing employee* on the grounds of race or sex, by:

1. The way opportunities for promotion, transfer, training or other benefits are provided, including deliberately omitting a person access to these (such as providing a particular training course only for whites, which then means that they have better promotion prospects).

2. Dismissals (such as dismissing more female than male workers in a particular job just because they are female).

3. Subjecting a person to any other detriment (i.e. anything which is directly or indirectly discriminatory).

Male or Female: How to Avoid Sex Discrimination

According to the Sex Discrimination Act, discrimination occurs when a woman is treated less favourably than a man because of her sex. The same definition of discrimination broadly applies to men.

These provisions have many practical implications for when you are selecting. You can see that you have to be very careful not to fall foul of the law at all stages of the process, and especially when:

- Deciding on the person specification (the criteria)
- Drawing up the shortlist
- Conducting the interview
- Making job offers

All this applies equally to race as well as to sex discrimination. Let's concentrate first on the interview.

Fair interviews

You should take care not to ask discriminatory questions in the interview. You must not ask questions that treat a female candidate less favourably than a male. Here is a list of some discriminatory questions you might be tempted to ask a woman candidate. *Avoid anything remotely like the following:*

Do you intend to have a family in the near future?
Do you think women are suited to this type of work?
I see you are engaged to be married. Does that mean you will be moving away from the area?
I note that you call yourself Ms. Why is that?
Do you think you would be able to gain the respect of males who report to you?
Are you legally separated?
How will you manage if the children are ill?
How will you manage about your children if you have to work late unexpectedly?
How would you deal with a man who made it clear that he didn't like having a woman boss?
How likely is your husband to move his job?

The reason these questons, and others like them, are discriminatory is because they're based on stereotyped views of women, their personalities, their abilities and capabilities, their work and their lives in general. The interviewer is treating a female candidate less favourably than a male by assuming that:

women cannot gain the respect of male subordinates,
  or
women are not suited to this type of work,
  or
a woman always follows her partner if he gets another job,
  or
women are the only ones who raise families,
  or
he is discriminating because of the biological fact that only women give birth.

As a rough and ready guide, you should ask yourself the question: 'Would I ask this question of a man?' If the answer is no, then you are probably asking a discriminatory question.

Also as a guide, always try to ask male and female candidates similar types of questions. That is not to say that you can never vary a set of questions from one interviewee to the next. But make sure that the differences in questions are based on factors other than gender.

Making job offers

You should be very careful about appointing someone whose experience or qualifications are considerably worse than those of another candidate of the opposite sex. You might claim that the interview performance of the favoured candidate far outweighed any lack of qualifications. Yet it is easy for someone to assume that the *real* reason you appointed that person was gender. You would have to support the claim of 'superior performance at the interview' with concrete examples. Not easy. Virtually impossible without evidence of previously decided upon, fair yardsticks to separate candidates. Moreover, these yardsticks or standards should be measurable.

It is a good idea to make notes during the interview (see Chapter 6) and to keep them for at least six months. Then, if needs be, you can use them as supporting evidence that you made the decision on proper evidence, not on the basis of the candidate's sex. The same goes for test scores and the results of any other assessment method you decide to use.

Married or single?

You are breaking the law if you discriminate against someone just because they are married. This was not always the case. Less than fifty years ago a woman had to give up her teaching post if she got married.

Fortunately, obvious prejudice like this is consigned to the history books. Take banking. For centuries, only men were allowed to have bank accounts. The Midland Bank, for example, had its first married female customer only 100 years ago. Now women account for half the bank's customers.

But less obvious discrimination against married women in employment may still exist and is illegal. As an employer, you must not treat a married person less favourably than a single person. For example, you are acting unlawfully if you appoint a single woman, rather than a young married woman, to a job just because the married woman might later leave to have a child.

Indirect sex discrimination

It is also discriminatory to make an unjustifiable job requirement which a smaller proportion of women than men can satisfy. This is indirect discrimination. 'Unjustifiable' means that the condition or requirement is not essential to effectively carrying out the job itself. An example is if you insisted that all job holders must stay in a job for a certain number of years. You should not draw up a shortlist, select or appoint on this basis. This is because it is likely to discriminate against young female candidates who might leave the job to have a family.

There are a number of exceptions to the provisions. These are where being a man or woman is a *genuine* occupational requirement or qualification. The exceptions are few, but the Act gives some guidelines. One is where the job needs to be held by one sex rather than another to preserve decency and privacy. An example is a changing-room attendant at a swimming baths. Another is where the nature of the place of work (a hospital or prison, for example) means that the supervision of those in care or detention are all of one sex and it is reasonable that the job should not be held by a person of the opposite sex. A final example is where the job must be held by a man because of legal restrictions on the employment of women. Such cases have a curious fascination but are rare. Mining is the best example; the Employment Protection Law of 1842 prevents women and children from working underground. (Incidentally, in November 1988 the Minister for Employment made a statement in the House of Commons proposing to change this law to allow women to become miners.)

Black or White: How to Avoid Race Discrimination

Just as with sex discrimination legislation, the Race Relations Act, 1976, makes it unlawful for an employer to treat one applicant less favourably than another, this time on racial grounds. The same goes for existing employees. 'Racial' in this context means race, colour, nationality or ethnic origins.

Deciding on the person specification

Firstly, you should carefully establish the person specification, or the criteria for selection (see Chapter 2). You must also make sure that they are objective and fair; you must not reach decisions in a subjective or arbitrary way.

One you have decided on criteria, you should select the best candidate according to them. The courts are getting more and more critical about sloppy selection practices which give full rein to subjectivity. This can allow discrimination to occur, or make it impossible to prove that it hasn't.

One case in 1988 concerned a black applicant who was discriminated against when applying for a senior nursing position. Although well qualified for the post, he was not even interviewed. The courts pointed to the lack of criteria when the employer, an Area Health Authority, drew up the shortlist.

Another recent example concerns a female Sri Lankan doctor. She was better qualified for the job than the other candidates, but she was not appointed. The courts took a dim view of the lack of objective selection criteria and she won her claim of discrimination. (See Box 1.)

BOX 1

The importance of objective criteria

The case involved the appointment of a doctor. There were three candidates, two white and a Sri Lankan. The person appointed was one of the white doctors, despite the fact that this candidate had published no research and had never held a hospital position. The Sri Lankan doctor gained the lowest interview grade of the three, despite her experience and a lot of published research to her name.

The reasons given by the appointments committee for rejecting the Sri Lankan doctor was that she lacked the training and experience. Then they said she was too academic. Then they said they had been looking for a candidate who was 'right', who would 'fit in', and who had 'stability', not just the best qualified.

Not surprisingly, the tribunal took the view that these were no criteria for selection, the decision had been reached in an arbitrary and subjective way, and that the appointments committee had preferred the white doctor. The Court of Appeal upheld the tribunal's decision and awarded compensation.

Noone v North West Thames Area Health Authority (1988 IDS Brief 376, IRLIB 352)

Fair interviews

The workings of the Act mean that you must take great care not to discriminate when you interview. *Absolutely avoid questions such as the following:*

Do you intend to return to the West Indies (Pakistan, India, Ireland, etc)?
What problems do you think you might find from members of the public? (implication: because you are black)
Do you think you'll be able to fit in with white colleagues?
Why do you call yourself British, with an accent like that? (an awful question, but it has been asked)
Would you, like so many other Indians I have employed in the past, keep wanting long holidays to go back to India?
Do you think our white employees would resent having a black boss?
Being Irish, are you going to lose your temper if annoyed with your fellow workers?
We like our employees to look smart. Do you have to wear a turban and beard?
Most of our Pakistani workers are manual workers. What special qualities do you have to be considered for this manager's job?
What makes you believe that this company will hire any more coloured people?

These questions, and others like them, are certain to be interpreted as treating the candidate less favourably than other applicants because of race. The golden rule is, ask similar questions of each applicant, regardless of race or ethnic origin. You must have an excellent reason, not related to race, for asking different questions of different applicants.

It should go without saying that more obvious forms of discrimination, such as refusing to offer a job to someone because of that person's race, are illegal under the Act.

Indirect racial discrimination

Indirect racial discrimination is also unlawful. This is where you apply the same selection requirement to everyone, but where one racial group is much more likely to be able to comply, and it cannot be justified. This means that you should not exclude candidates by laying down criteria which fewer minority applicants (Black, Asian, foreign, etc) can satisfy. So, insisting that successful candidates should not live in Liverpool 8 district would be considered discriminatory because a much greater proportion of the population there is coloured (around 50%) than is the case in the rest of Merseyside (where the proportion is around 2%).

Similarly, if you said that all trainee representatives should be at least six feet tall, or have blond hair, that would be indirect discrimination, since certain races are much more likely to be able to meet this rule, and the rule has no justification. Incidentally, the six foot rule would also be indirect sex discrimination.

The Race Relations Act, just like the Sex Discrimination Act, does allow what might on the surface seem like favourable treatment for one sector of the community. This is only if it is justifiable for the job. So, you might be within the law if you insisted that an applicant can speak Urdu even though less white applicants than Asians would be able to fulfil this particular requirement. But this would only be lawful if the job you were offering involved extensive work with Asians.

How to Write Non-Discriminatory Advertisements

You are no doubt also aware that adverts can indicate discrimination. You should take care that the job titles and the language used in advertisements do not contain a sexual or racial message. To advertise for the job of 'Headmaster' presumably means that women can't apply and so is discriminatory. You should use the word 'Headteacher' instead. Watch out for words like salesman, barmaid, waiter, cleaning lady, charwoman, postman or storeman. Make sure you write the advert to show clearly that both sexes can apply.

There are also more subtle forms of discrimination in advertisements. This is where jobs have been traditionally done by one sex, such as typist, mechanic, pilot, or office cleaner. Again, your

BOX 2 (i)

A Discriminatory Advertisement

WAITER
required

No experience necessary

Apply:
Grubb's Restaurant
Station Road
Mulberry Hill
Higgingtown

BOX 2 (ii)

A Non-Discriminatory Advertisement

WAITER/WAITRESS
required

No experience necessary

Apply:
Grubb's Restaurant
Station Road
Mulberry Hill
Higgingtown

advert should show that both sexes can apply. Use phrases like 'mechanic, male or female'.

Finally, you must alternate 'he' and 'she', 'her' and 'him', throughout the advert, such as by having 'he/she' or 'she or he'. Alternatively, avoid them altogether. Either way, it is obvious that you mean that both men and women can apply.

Ethnic and Sex Monitoring

Both the Commission for Racial Equality and the Equal Opportunities Commission codes of practice recommend sex and ethnic monitoring. This means that you should keep records of the progress of the sexes and of different racial groups in the workforce. I've included some simple record forms, designed by the Commission for Racial Equality, in this chapter (Figures 12.1, 12.2 and 12.3). I strongly recommend that you use them to keep a watch on the balance in your workforce.

At this point you may be thinking that monitoring seems like discrimination in action. But there are two main reasons why it is important for you to keep such records. The benefits of doing so far outweigh the risks that the information could be used to foster and encourage discrimination.

1. Morally, you have a duty to see to it that your employees of whatever race and either gender are treated fairly. The only sure way of knowing if this is the case is to keep records. In particular, it allows you to monitor the number of people making it into the more attractive levels of the organization (breaking what has been called 'The Glass Ceiling').

2. The second reason is pragmatic and defensive. If someone brings a discrimination case against you, you will need to have the factual, written evidence that your employment practices have been fair to different sectors of the workforce.

Figure 12.4 gives a list of employment activities that you need to monitor.

Courts getting tougher on racial discrimination

In the past, it has not always been easy for applicants to prove racial discrimination against them. But a Court of Appeal ruling in 1988 has made life easier for claimants. The ruling, as you might expect, is a bit of a mouthful but here goes. The Court

Specifically related to recruitment and selection

Wording, presentation and media used for advertising
Responses to advertising
Shortlisting from returned application forms
Interviewing
Offers of employment
Acceptance of offers of employment
Job specifications and criteria for employment

General employment conditions

Reviews of probationary periods
Terms and conditions
Promotions
Re-gradings
Transfers
Disciplinary procedures
Grievance procedures
Dismissals
Leavers
Reasons for leaving
Access to and take up of training opportunities
Existing staff

Adapted from: Carr, J. 'Comments on monitoring,' in: *Record Keeping and Monitoring in Education and Employment*, London: Runnymead Trust (1980).

Figure 12.4 List of Employment Activities that need to be Monitored

stated that if an applicant could show that an employer had treated a particular racial group less favourably than another, then any less favourable treatment given to an applicant is caused by the fact that he or she is a member of that racial group.

Let's try and rephrase that, in case the meaning is not crystal clear. Assume I'm an applicant for a job you are offering, and I feel I've been discriminated against by you. All I need do is:

1. Show that my racial group is already being treated less fairly than another in your company.

2. Show that I have not been given the job.
3. Claim the reason for this is unfairly related to my race.
4. Take you to a tribunal.

The Court also ruled that the employer should provide the applicant with the statistics that would prove whether his or her racial group was being treated less favourably.

You will see that the crux of the matter lies in the fact that you are already discriminating. This gives me good grounds for my claim as a failed candidate. So watch out. Look at your current workforce and current practices. And be certain that you are not discriminating now, or in later selection decisions.

Have a look at Box 3 on page 189 for a real example. Then, if you want, you can test yourself on a discrimination law quiz. Have a go.

Form A: Distribution of Employees by Ethnic Group

Industrial Employees Section .... Date ....

	BLACK				WHITE		
Origin:	Afro-Caribbean	African	Asian	Other	European (Including UK)	Other	TOTAL
Maintenance							
Engineers							
Production Workers:							
Grade A							
B							
C							
D							
E							
Despatch							
Chargehands							
Supervisors							

Industrial Employees Section .... Date ....

	BLACK				WHITE		
Origin:	Afro-Caribbean	African	Asian	Other	European (Including UK)	Other	TOTAL
Typists							
Secretaries							
Clerical Staff:							
Grade: A							
B							
C							
Supervisory							
Managerial							
Technical/ Professional							

Figure 12.1

Form B: Recruitment Records

Date of Application	Name/Address of Applicant	Ethnic Origins	Post Applied for	Result of Application	Reason for rejection (where appropriate)

Note: A similar form might be used for applications for internal upgrading, training, promotion, etc.

Figure 12.2

Form C: Analysis of Recruitment Statistics Period from .... to ....

		BLACK				WHITE		
		Afro-Caribbean Origin	African Origin	Asian Origin	Other	European Origin (including UK)	Other	TOTAL
	(a) (b)	Number applied/ engaged	Number applied/ engaged	Number applied/ engaged	Number applied/ engaged	Number applied/ engaged	Number applied/ engaged	Number applied/ engaged
Industrial employees								
Maintenance	(a)							
	(b)							
Production (according to grade)	(a)							
	(b)							
Despatch	(a)							
	(b)							
Supervisory	(a)							
	(b)							
TOTAL	(a)							
	(b)							

Note: A similar report/summary form might be used for internal upgrading, training, promotion, etc.

Figure 12.3

BOX 3

The importance of ethnic monitoring

The case involved an Asian, Mr Singh, who had worked for a bus company for many years. He had started as a bus driver and later became an inspector. In 1985, the company invited inspectors to apply for the position of senior inspector. Fifty-five applied; twenty-six made it to the shortlist, including Mr Singh and three other coloured inspectors. Nine inspectors were promoted, all of whom were white. Mr Singh, supported by the Commission for Racial Equality (CRE), claimed racial discrimination.

The employer had an equal opportunities policy in force since 1983, and had been monitoring manual jobs, including inspectors, since 1984. It provided details of the fifty-five candidates, including ethnic origins, qualifications, managers' reports and decision letters. Mr Singh wanted more than this. He asked the company to produce details of the ethnic origins of people who had applied for, or been appointed to, posts within a band of grades similar to that of senior inspector.

At the industrial tribunal stage, the company was ordered to produce these statistics. The company objected. The case then went to the Court of Appeal, who rejected the employer's appeal.

The lesson from this is that industrial tribunals have wide powers to order the disclosure of relevant information. The information requested by Mr Singh was relevant because it might show that his racial group had been subjected to discrimination. If it did, then the tribunal could infer that the company had discriminated against Mr Singh.

Monitoring is part of the CRE code. So, if any employer doesn't bother to monitor, then a claim that no discrimination has taken place is likely to be looked on with scepticism by a tribunal.

West Midlands Passenger Transport Executive v Singh
(1988 IRLR 186, IDS Brief 373).

BOX 4

Discrimination Law Quiz

Instructions

For each of the following questions, see if you think it is unlawful discrimination or not. When you have done them all, look over the page for the answers.

Race discrimination questions

1. A tractor manufacturer in the West Midlands wants to draw up a shortlist of candidates for jobs. So they look in their filing cabinets and bring out all the unsolicited letters of application they have recently received. They give special attention to those who had submitted a letter of application in good English, who talk about their experience, their qualifications and the sort of work they want. The shortlist is based on these letters.

Unlawful discrimination? YES/NO

2. Mr A., a West Indian, applies for a job as a waiter in a Chinese restaurant. He is turned down on the grounds that all the waiters are Chinese and only Chinese food is served.

Unlawful discrimination? YES/NO

3. Ms B. is of black African origin. She applies for a job as a manager in a company whose main customer is a South African firm which regularly sends representatives over to the factory. One of the jobs of the new manager would be to look after the South African visitors. She is turned down because it is felt that they would object to the fact that she is black.

Unlawful discrimination? YES/NO

4. An English local government officer who applies for a job in Wales. All the people in the area speak English but the local

authority are anxious to promote the use of the Welsh language and will only consider a Welsh speaker.

Unlawful discrimination? YES/NO

5. Mr D. is a Sikh whose religion forbids him to shave off his beard. He applies for a job in a food factory, but is rejected because all employees must be clean shaven.

Unlawful discrimination? YES/NO

6. A Muslim claims that he should be entitled to paid leave for Muslim holidays, like Christians, but the employer thinks otherwise.

Unlawful discrimination? YES/NO

7. Ms E., born in London, applies for a job as a trainee in a company which has an associate company in Belgium. She does not get an interview because she is told that the job had been reserved for a trainee from the Belgian factory who will work at the factory and then return to Belgium after completing the training.

Unlawful discrimination? YES/NO

Sex discrimination questions

8. A woman applies for a job in the Executive grade of the Civil Service. She is not appointed. The reason given is that she is over the age limit of twenty-eight for first entry.

Unlawful discrimination? YES/NO

9. Ms G. applies for a job as sales assistant in a Menswear shop. The manager refuses to consider a woman because the job involves taking inside leg measurements.

Unlawful discrimination? YES/NO

10. Mr H. applies for a job in a travel agency. During the interview he reveals that his wife works for a rival firm. He does not get the job because the employer feels there would be a high risk of loss of confidentiality which would be detrimental for business.

Unlawful discrimination? YES/NO

11. Ms P. applies for a job as a manager at a garden centre. The man who runs the garden centre writes to tell her that he will not consider her or any woman for the post because the job involves carrying heavy and bulky items, such as bags of peat. He says later that, in any case, there were other applicants with more experience than Ms P. Was his rejection of Ms P's application lawful?

Unlawful discrimination? YES/NO

12. While on maternity leave having her second child, Ms J. writes to her employers asking if she can return to work on a part-time basis. She maintains that, as a single parent, she will have difficulty coping with a full-time job and that she can see no practical job difficulties if she is allowed to work part-time. Her request is refused.

Unlawful discrimination? YES/NO

ANSWERS

Race discrimination

1. YES. it is indirect discrimination.
The reason is that it gives an unfair advantage to those who knew about the firm, its vacancies and its recruitment policies. They could find this out from existing employees. Since nearly all the existing employees were white, and because these mostly told other white people, the result of this recruitment method was to exclude black applicants. Not surprisingly, the tractor company had only a very few black workers despite being in an area where a good number of blacks lived.
Massey Ferguson Perkins Ltd, Report of a Formal Investigation, Commission for Racial Equality, 1982.

2. NO. Employers in catering or entertainment can restrict jobs to applicants of a particular ethnic background in the interests of authenticity. However if Mr A. had applied for a job as a chef in the restaurant kitchen where he would not have been seen by the customers, then the grounds for not employing him would not have been justified.

3. YES. An employer cannot justify discrimination by showing that his customers or employees are prejudiced, even if he could prove that his business would suffer as a result of employing someone like Ms B.

4. YES. An employer cannot set a language requirement that is not essential for the job. Similarly, if an employer refuses a job, say, to a Pakistani on the grounds that his or her English is not good enough, then the employer would need to satisfy a tribunal that a good knowledge of English was necessary for that particular job and that the language requirement had not been imposed to keep out non-white applicants.

5. NO. the requirement forbidding beards was justified on the grounds of hygiene. However, employers must be sure that the requirements are justifiable and not just an excuse for discrimination.

6. NO. A tribunal would probably reject the claim on the grounds that Muslims are not a racial group. Although they have some of the characteristics, such as common culture, historic traditions and background, they do not have others like language and shared nationality.
Niaz v Ryman Ltd (1988 IDS Brief 376; IT).

7. NO. The Race Relations Act makes special provisions for the education or training of people who do not live in the U.K. and who intend to leave the country after their education or training.

Sex discrimination

8. YES. An Employment Appeal Tribunal judged this to be indirect discrimination and found in the woman's favour. The age limit of twenty-eight is unfair to women since this is the age when many women are bearing and raising children. If you impose an age limit, you should consider whether the age bar has a significantly greater effect on one sex over another within the pool of likely candidates for the job. If it does then it is probably unlawful.
Price v Civil Service Commission and Society of Civil and Public Servants, 1976

9. YES. Although discrimination is allowed in jobs for which the sex of the worker is a 'Genuine Occupation Qualification', such cases are limited and in this case would not be allowed. The male customers would be able to preserve their decency by trying on their trousers in the privacy of a changing cubicle. For the few customers who require their inside leg to be measured there are male sales assistants available.

10. NO. The fact that Mr H. did not get the job was because of the risk posed to the business and would equally well have applied if he had been a woman. Therefore the decision was not due to sex discrimination. Also the risk of the 'leaking' of confidential information could arise as much between non-married people of close association as between married people and therefore there was no marriage discrimination.

11. YES. Even though there were other reasons why Ms P. might not have been given the job, the main reason for her rejection was obviously the fact that she was a woman. If she had been interviewed and had shown that she was not up to the heavy lifting, this would have been a different matter.

12. YES. The condition to work full-time was to Ms J.'s detriment and she could only comply with it by putting herself under a severe disadvantage. The requirement to work full time had a serious detrimental effect.

(You should note that this is a very particular case, because of Ms J.'s particular difficulties, and stands very much on its own.)

Key points

1. The Sex Discrimination Act and Race Relations Act make direct and indirect sex and race discrimination at work unlawful.

2. Indirect discrimination is where you apply the same selection requirement to eveyone, but where one sex or racial group is more likely to be able to comply, and it cannot be justified.

3. Nor must you discriminate against women because they are married.

4. Pay particular attention to:

   - Job requirements
   - Fair criteria for selecting who will be interviewed
   - Making sure interviews are carried out in the same way for all candidates
   - Making selection as objective as possible by using verifiable facts and performance measures

5. Advertisements should be carefully phrased so as not to imply discrimination, e.g. waiter should be waiter/waitress, salesgirl

should be sales person. Make it clear that jobs normally done by one sex (such as mechanic) are open to both sexes.

6. You should monitor the selection and promotion of women and racial groups in the workforce.

13 Putting What You've Learned to Work

'The great end of life is not knowledge but action.'

T. H. Huxley

Selecting a secretary

If you are still with me at this point in the book, you will have read about, and hopefully learnt some new things about:

Job descriptions
Person specifications
Application forms
Interviewing
Testing
Telling candidates about the job
Work samples
In-tray exercises
Sex and race discrimination
. . . and many more

Now it's time to put what you've read into practice.

Imagine that your secretary has just announced that she is leaving. Even if the very thought gives you apoplexy, just pause for a moment and think through the steps of replacing her. The more important ones are:

Job description
Person specification
Advertisement
Screening

Interviewing
Testing
Making the decision

I suggest that you go through each of these stages in turn and get some practice in selection. Obviously I can't make it totally realistic. I can't, for example, arrange for you to really interview some candidate secretaries, but treat this as a dry run. Better to make a few mistakes here than when you have to do it for real.

Job Description

Make a list of all those tasks your present secretary does for you and your organization. If you don't have a secretary right now, think of the tasks the lucky person you propose to recruit will do! Then structure these tasks in the following framework.

Job title
Main purpose of the job
Position in the organization
- Who the job holder reports to
- Who reports to the job holder

Key tasks or results areas
- Scope of the job
- Limits of authority

Any other information

The most important of these categories is 'key tasks'. Give most thought to this.

When you have finished you will have comc a fair way towards writing a professional job description. A useful idea might be to ask your secretary to produce a similar list and compare it with yours.

If you get stuck, turn to Chapter 2 and look again at descriptions.

I have written a typical job description for a secretary, reproduced on the next page. Hopefully yours looks similar, though I certainly don't expect it to look the same. Your secretary will have a different job from mine. Check, though, to see that you haven't missed out something important.

Your job description of a secretary

Secretarial Job Description (Summary)

Job title
Secretary/personal asistant to the managing director.

Main purpose of the job
To provide a full range of secretarial services for the MD of a 5-person management consultancy firm. There is occasional work for other consultants and directors.

Position in the organization
The job holder will report to the MD.
There are 4 consultants, and one other secretary.

Key tasks
The duties are mainly administrative. They cover a wide variety of responsibilities including:

- Dealing with incoming and outgoing mail
- Arranging meetings.
- Arranging travel
- Making appointments and keeping the MD's engagement diary
- Keeping simple accounting records on such matters as fee-earning days, expenses, VAT, invoices, bills outstanding, etc
- Typing of correspondence, technical reports. All typing is done on a word processor, and typing forms approximately 10% of the job
- There is an occasional need for shorthand and audio-typing
- Researching in libraries and databases
- The job holder will work on his/her own initiative for a large part of the work

Conditions of service
The basic arrangement is for a 35-hour week.
Starting and finishing times are open to negotiation, and can be arranged to suit parents with responsibilities for children.
Salary is £7,500 for a 35-hour week.
Holidays are 23 days per year.

Person Specification

Now that you have laid out what your secretary does, and how, the next step is to write a person specification. You will remember that this is an outline of the job in 'people terms'. It tells you what you need to look for in candidates.

I suggest you use a seven- or eight-point plan as a framework. See Chapter 2, if in doubt.

Again, have a go yourself first. Then have a look at my attempt over the page.

Your Person Specification of a Secretary

Person Specification: Secretary

Essential Characteristics

Physical
Articulate
Clear speech
Neat and tidy appearance

Attainments
Shorthand: Minimum 100 wmp (Pitmans or equivalent)
Typing: Minimum 50 wmp (RSA Stage III or equivalent)
English Language at GCE O-level (or equivalent, e.g. CSE Grade 1; RSA Stage III; GCSE)
Word Processor experience: Word Perfect 4.2 trained, or minimum 6 months' experience
2 years secretarial experience
Driving licence

Aptitudes
Good with words (oral and written)
Good telephone manner
Sound basic arithmetic

Interests
None in particular

Disposition
Acceptable to others
Self reliant
Sense of humour
Personable (enjoys, and is capable of, mixing with a wide variety of people)
Dependable
Tact

Motivation
Successful candidate will be motivated by pleasant and friendly environment, and by being of service to others.

Circumstances
The job calls for a man or woman living within reasonable travelling distance of the workplace and willing to work occasional overtime.

Salary scale
£5,500–£6,500 (dependent on age and experience).

Advertisement

With the job description and the person specification done, you are now ready to write an advertisement.

Decide how many hours you want him/her to work and how much you are prepared to pay.

Decide which newspaper you will put the advertisement in. Or you might decide to use one of the other outlets I have talked about, such as the local employment agency or Job Centre.

Remember to phrase the advertisement carefully – you don't want to be accused of discrimination.

Again, once you have had a go, take a look over the page at my effort. Your advert will probably look something similar.

Your Advertisement

ADVERTISEMENT

SHACKLETON ENTERPRISES

Secretarial Vacancies

Shackleton Enterprises will shortly have a vacancy for a

FULL-TIME SECRETARY
(Male or Female)

The secretary/assistant will work for a small group of tutors and business consultants. The work is varied and includes:

Typing correspondence, reports, etc
Keeping staff diaries
Extensive telephoning
Arranging meetings and taking minutes
Organizing courses
Library research

Successful candidates are likely to have shorthand speeds of 100 wmp (Pitmans or equivalent), RSA Stage III typewriting or equivalent, and experience with word processors. A starting salary around £8,000 per annum is offered.

Hours of work are 09.00–17.00 hours Monday to Friday.

Application form from:

Dr V. J. Shackleton
Shackleton Enterprises Ltd
Littletown
West Midlands

Tel.: Littletown 1234

Screening: sifting the applications

Application forms

Next, you'll need to send each enquirer an application form. You could use one of those in Chapter 5.

Let's assume you have received a dozen or more completed forms. This is far too many for the shortlist, so you need to get the number down. The only sensible way to do it is to compare the applicants' qualifications and experience with the person specification.

The best way is to draw up a brief checklist based on the person specification. Take each application and tick those items where they meet the requirements. Those who have few ticks, and so don't fit the bill, you should screen out.

References

You could verify the shortlisted candidates application data, and possibly find out extra information, from previous employers (assuming there are any). As you will know by now, I'm lukewarm about the idea, feeling that it will tell you little of use. If you do take up references, I suggest you use the telephone not a letter. And use a checklist such as the one in Chapter 7.

Rejections

Write to those whom you reject, thanking them for their interest.

Interviewing

Now you will want to interview the most suitable applicants. Design the interview format in detail, deciding who will be involved in the interviewing, what questions you will want asked, etc. Remember to use open-ended questions wherever possible, particularly at the beginning.

It might be useful to make a list of prejudices that you are not going to take into account, especially if, like most of us, you have certain hobby horses which would not be relevant to the selection procedure in hand.

Take a look over the page at some of my questions. Yours will probably include some similar ones.

Some Interview questions when selecting a secretary

Work experience

You worked as a secretary in company X. What did this job involve?
Why did you take the job?
Why did you leave?
Which parts of the job did you like best? Which parts did you like least? Why was that?
How much did you have to rely on your own initiative? Can you give me some examples?
What were the sort of work problems you came across? How did you deal with them?
What were your colleagues like?

Skills and training

What secretarial skills do you have?
What are your typing/shorthand speeds?
Can you audio type?
What skills and abilities do you think are important in a secretary? Can you give me some examples of where you have had to use these skills in you work?

Motivation

What are you looking for in this job?
Why would you like to work here?
Where do you see yourself in five years' time?
What sort of work do you best enjoy?

Testing

We will assume that you are not going to give the applicants a whole series of tests, but you may want to give a few work samples. Jot down what type of work you will include in these samples.

Yours may well have included:

Typing and page layouts
Word processing
Shorthand
Telephone manner

Preferably they should be standardized ones such as:

ACER Short clerical test
ACER Speed and accuracy test
SHL Automated office battery
SHL Eosys word processing aptitude battery
SHL Personnel test battery, including checking and classification (filing)
SRA office skills tests
SRA typing tests

(See Appendix for suppliers of these tests)

Making the decision

You should base your decision of which person to appoint on the evidence you have now amassed. These data you will have collected from the application form, references, interview and work samples.

How to compare the facts and impressions is now the problem. It may be that one person will stand head and shoulders above the others. This is unlikely, though, if you have had a good pool of applicants to start with.

The best method for comparing the candidates is the matrix approach I talked about in the practical exercise in Chapter 4. You will remember that this involves putting the attributes you have considered down the left-hand side of the page and the candidates along the top. Then you can systematically compare each candidate on each criterion. For example, you might have typing speed, shorthand speed, motivation, personality, able to work overtime occasionally, and so on, down the left-hand side. Give a score to how well each candidate performed on these criteria. It is very similar to the chart of Chapter 4, which you might like to look at again now.

Conclusions

No one pretends that assessing people and making selection decisions is easy. It is a truism that people are complex and difficult to fathom, let alone predict what they will do when they work for us.

What I hope this exercise, and the book as a whole, has done is to help you systematically think through the steps and techniques that are needed to make a good job of picking people for jobs. It may have forced you to reconsider the methods you currently use. It may have prompted you to try using methods you hadn't seriously considered before when you come to do it the next time. It may just have given you the warm glow of knowing that you were doing it right all along.

One thing is for sure. Nobody ever gets selection right every time. I fondly remember hearing of a distinguished assessment consultant and academic who helped a firm recruit a senior official. Three years later the executive absconded to South America, having swindled his employer out of millions.

What we can all hope to do is be a little more professional in our approach to recruitment and selection. This involves selecting with the best methods available and using them fairly. That way we increase our chances of getting it right more often than we get it wrong.

I hope this chapter and this book will help you next time you come to the tricky task of selection.

Good luck!

Appendix

Case Study: *Selection of Sales People in a Financial Services Company*

'I often quote myself.
It adds spice to my conversation.'
George Bernard Shaw

Background

A finance company wanted to improve the way it selected sales people, called New Business Representatives.

Most finance companies are owned by banks and their business is to lend money. They provide the finance for major purchases like cars or furniture, and home improvement such as kitchen units or double glazing. The job of sales person in companies like this is to sell money. Typically, they don't place business (i.e. arrange the supply of finance) directly with the individual, the person like you or me who wants to buy a new car, say, but with the shop or company we buy from.

Say you want to treat yourself to some new bedroom furniture. You've had your eye on it for a long while, but there's a problem – a 'temporary shortage of liquidity'. No problem, says the shop assistant. The shop can arrange finance for you. This is where the finance house comes in. The company they recommend is the finance house they have chosen to do business with.

The reason this particular finance company wanted to look at the selection of its new business representatives was that the nature of the job had changed a great deal over the recent few years. Prior to that they had been losing sales people. But a well-designed selection procedure had brought labour turnover to acceptable levels. However, with the changes in the nature of the job, and the context in which it was carried out, the old methods of selection were becoming suspect. The company was concerned that they might be recruiting people who were ideally suited to the *old* job which in reality no longer existed. The job title, New Business Representative, remained but the nature of the job, its tasks, duties and responsibilities, had changed dramatically. What they wanted now were people best suited to the new, presently existing, job.

As an important aside, I said that previously the turnover of people was unacceptably high. This immediately begs the question of why a high leaving rate translates into a selection problem. There are lots of reasons why people quit an employer. Being in the wrong job is only one of them. Other reasons include wanting more money, moving out of the area, domestic reasons like pregnancy, retirement, lack of opportunities for promotion, as well as a host of others.

Suffice it to say that the company were fairly certain in this case that the issue had to do with selection. They knew this from the nature of those who had left. These people tended to be those who could not cope with the training, or who had to be dismissed for being unsuitable for the work. They tended not to be those who left for better jobs or for domestic reasons. While sales jobs typically have higher leaving rates than many other jobs, when compared with the finance industry average, the company were convinced that their failure rate was worse than average.

Design of the Study

The study was designed to:

- Find out what changes had taken place in the job over time
- Identify the critical components that separate good reps from less good ones
- Make recommendations for selecting reps

The study involved interviewing presently involved representatives. It is important in a study like this not to alarm the interviewees. They need to be reassured that their own jobs are not under threat.

Consequently, the company sent a memo to all those who were to be asked to participate in the study. Part of it read:

> 'Due to the many changes that have taken place in the role of the New Business Representative, it is felt that the selection procedures for applicants should be amended and brought up to date.
>
> We would like you to participate in this exercise which will necessitate spending half a day with the researcher. We hasten to add that your participation in no way affects your present or future position with the Company and the information you provide will be used purely as a guide based on your experience.'

Collecting Information

Interviews were held with eight New Business Representatives employed by the company. The youngest was twenty-six, the oldest forty-two; their length of experience ranged from two to nine years, and they were drawn from separate branches. In addition, two Assistant Branch Managers who had worked previously as representatives were interviewed. So was a Regional Manager, to provide an overview of the job.

Each research interview lasted from two to three hours. The aim was to gather information about the job content and the setting in which the job was performed.

Repertory grids were used during the interviews to get at specific types of information. This method was mentioned in Chapter 2 and involves comparing various features of the job, or people who do the job, with one another, so as to get at the major differences.

The first task was to look to see whether the business environment had changed in ways that might affect the job and, if so, in what ways.

For the repertory grids, the interviewees were asked to think of occasions concerned with:

Previous business (five years ago)
Present business
Future business (five years into the future)

Next they were asked to describe them. Then they compared one with the other by talking about their differences from each other and then the similarities.

The respondents were asked to give an adjective or phrase which summarized the difference or similarity they had in mind.

Results

a) Changes in the business environment

From this kind of exercise we can draw up a grid. This describes the key differences and similarities in the nature of the business between the present, the future and the past, as seen by the people who know the job.

From this initial analysis, shown in Table A.1, it is clear that there have been major changes in the nature of the business, and more are expected. This is according to those who are currently doing the job, and they should know. These changes are a trend away from selling mostly finance for car purchases, to a much wider range of purposes for the loan. There has also been a shift from the business coming in almost automatically, to the need to go out and canvass, prospect, and be more professional. These changes are expected to continue. In particular, the sales reps think that there will be greater opportunities provided by a wider range of types of lending, a greater geographical spread and by others, who will increasingly refer business their way.

On the down side, they also expect greater threats. The business environment is expected to get tougher, with increasing competition, especially from building societies.

b) Changes in representatives' jobs

It was obvious from this initial study that the business changes had led to shifts in the nature of the representatives' jobs. This implies

Present business

Development of home improvement loan market
More competitive
More customer-orientated
More professional service with loans geared to new reasons for people needing money
Pro-active to market
More versatility

The business five years ago

Differences from present
Traditional HP market in motor trade
Passive
Servicing
Reactive to the market
Change in legislation

Similarities to present
Always market for borrowing
Company a market leader
Advertising
Use of brokers
Negotiations

The business in five years' time

Differences from present
Greater commercialism
Fierce competition from Building Societies
Geographical spread from branch
Product sophistication, e.g. warranties
Explorative markets, e.g. commercial loans, leasing, first mortgages
Referrals

Similarities to present
New markets in home improvement stabilizing
Legislation
Cold canvassing
Negotiation

Table A.1: Changes in the business

that the company needs to look for different requirements in reps, especially when selecting them.

Interviews and repertory grids were again used to look for similarities and differences in individuals best suited to the changing business environment. Three bench-marks were used. These were:

Previous characteristics required of reps
Present characteristics
Future characteristics

Table A.2 shows the results.

This second analysis shows that in the future representatives will increasingly need to develop skills which make the requirements of the job different from the past.

For one thing, they need to be more competitive and aggressive in their search for business. They see this as an obvious follow-on from the increasingly competitive environment they find themselves in.

They also need greater commercial awareness and product knowledge, as well as an ability to cope with complexity. This stems from the increase in information which needs to be delved into, learnt and assimilated, and spiralling demand to know more and more about more and more businesses.

On a personal level, it looks like there is an increased emphasis on interpersonal skills such as communication, understanding others and making presentations.

c) Good and poor performers

A third and final grid was used to find out what distinguished the high, medium and low performer amongst New Business Representatives. This allows us to check out the earlier findings. It also gives us clues on what we should be looking for at selection time so as to increase the chance of getting a good performer rather than a poor one.

This time, interviewees were asked to think of three New

Present characteristics

Aggressive
Greater product knowledge
Developing and thinking for themselves
Selling
Persuasive
Greater adaptability
Prober
Listener
Decisive
Tutor

Characteristics five years ago

Differences from present:
Passive
Supportive
Trainer

Similarities to present:
Documenter
Processor
Servicer

Characteristics in five years' time

Differences from present:
Competitive
More aggressive
Commercial awareness
Product knowledge
Delver
Communicative
Coping with complexity
Analyse people

Similarities to present:
Business development skills
Presenter

Table A.2: Changes in characteristics of representatives

Business Reps they knew or had known. They were asked to choose a:

Very good performer
Mediocre performer
Bad performer

Once again, the repertory grid technique forces the interviewee who is providing the information to think about what is similar and different in these three individuals. Results for the good versus the poor performer are displayed in Table A.3.

Use of the results in selection

It is one thing to carefully and systematically discover what the job involves and what skills are needed to effectively carry out the job. It is a whole different question to move from this to designing a selection procuedure to assess these skills in candidates. And selection in itself is only one approach to the changes that have taken place in the business and the job. A second approach is to train existing job holders or new people coming in to the job. So the results can be used for both selection and training.

a) Testing
Compared with a few years earlier, the job now entails a great deal of learning. There is researching customers, learning about their businesses, product knowledge to mug up, legislation to be familiar with, masses of complexity to cope with, thinking things through for yourself, and a range of other areas where the sales person needs to be on the ball. Not surprisingly, the reps themselves said that intelligence separated the effective from the poor. So one obvious way of separating out the bright from the less bright at the selection stage is to use an intelligence or reasoning test. This is what was done. The level of reasoning demanded by the test was pitched at the level of the typical successful candidate.

Secondly, a personality questionnaire was used to tap some of the characteristics needed in the 'new' job. It measured those

Good performer
Feedback skills
Delegation skills
Very ambitious
Sense of purpose
Very determined
High drive
Sets goals
Good listener
High job commitment
Very good telephone manner
Takes corporate view
Very good at coping with pressure
Can occupy own time productively
Works well within a team
Up-to-date market knowledge
Poor performer
Emotional
Erratic
Lacks understanding of others
Mistrustful
Low job commitment
Lazy
Doesn't think things out for self
Misguided purpose
Not a good mixer in the office
Inaccurate
Believes in oneupmanship

Table A.3: The good versus the poor performer

characteristics needed at the present and in the future, such as creative thinking, assertiveness, and ability to cope with pressure.

b) Interviewing

In addition to testing, there are many implications from this research for how the interview should be conducted. We now know a great deal about what it takes to be successful in the job. So interviewers can look for evidence of these skills in candidates. An interview checklist was drawn up to help interviewers find evidence of previous successes at these skills and tasks.

Another way of using this information would be to design situational interviews (see Chapter 6), though this was not done here.

Use of the results in training

Training programmes were set up for both new and existing reps to help them learn the skills needed in the job. These included:

- Communicating ideas to an audience (e.g. presentation skills)
- Accurate administration
- Researching and collating information
- Probing for details in client meetings

Cheap self-paced training packages on general commercial knowledge, financial markets and methods, and business analysis could also be developed as part of the training and development programme.

Useful Addresses

British Institute of Management
Africa House
64–78 Kingsway
London WC2B 6BL
Tel.: 01-405 3456

British Psychological Society
St Andrews House
48 Princess Road East
Leicester LE1 7DR
Tel.: 0533 549568

Commission for Racial Equality
Elliot House
10–12 Allington Street
London SW1E 5EH
Tel.: 01-828 7022

Equal Opportunities Commission
Overseas House
Quay Street
Manchester M3 3HN
Tel.: 061-833 9244

Institute of Personnel Management
IPM House
Camp Road
Wimbledon
London SW19 4UW
Tel.: 01-946 9100

Books for Further Help

General Books on Selection

Smith, M. and Robertson, L. *The Theory and Practice of Systematic Staff Selection*. Macmillan, 1986.

A bible for those who want to get in deep into methods of selecting staff. Comprehensive, detailed and professional in approach. More a textbook than a cookbook. After reading this book, you can be sure that you know more about selection than 99% of managers, as well as more than a good proportion of assorted headhunters and other recruitment and selection consultants. Its insistence on the accepted academic style of quoting the source of each statement and research finding may put you off. It needs time and patience to get to grips with this book, but the results are worth it.

Cook, M. *Personnel Selection and Productivity*. John Wiley, 1988

A fairly easy to read book that contains a lot of sound advice. Some nice touches of humour. Rather academic in format, with lots of references to studies, but useful if you are seriously interested in getting to grips with how professional selection practice can make your business more productive.

Lewis, C. *Employee Selection*. Hutchinson, 1985

One of a series of books by Hutchinson in their Personnel Management series. Mostly aimed at the personnel manager, though can be read with profit by anybody concerned with selecting people. The first half of the book looks at the nature of recruitment and selection and some of the 'hot issues' in the field. The second half covers practices and principles of selection, with guidance on how to do it properly. Another excellent book to help you with selection.

Recruitment and Selection

Plumbley, P. *Recruitment and Selection*. Institute of Personnel Mangement, 4th edn, 1985.

This book has gone through numerous reprints and editions since it first saw the light of day in 1968. A short paperback with an intensely practical, no-nonsense approach. Covers recruitment ('attracting a field of candidates') and placement as well as selection, though the price you pay for this wider coverage is less depth on the topic of selection processes.

Sidney, E. (ed.) *Management Recruiting*. Gower, 1988.

A weighty book, which can be dipped into as required. Twenty-three chapters by different authors. Topics cover the whole gamut of recruitment as well as selection. Chapters range through manpower planning, the law, interviews and special categories of selection, such as sales people and graduates. A good, fairly comprehensive guidebook.

Books on Specific Topics

Job analysis

Pearn, M. and Kandola, R. *Job Analysis: A Practical Guide for Managers*. Institute of Personnel Management, 1988.

Another 'practical guide' published by the IPM, this time on the technical topic (sometimes considered rather boring topic) of job analysis. Looks at analysing the job, the task and the role (JTR) with a range of different techniques. Shows that the uses of JTR are not confined to selection, though many of the case studies illustrate the importance of JTR to making fair and competent selection decisions.

Job descriptions

Ungerson, B. *How to Write a Job Description*. Institute of Personnel Mangement, 1983.

A delightful, short, punchy little book. Tells you all you need to know about the topic, including examples of the good, the bad and the ugly.

Interviewing

There is a useful chapter on this in *Employee Selection* (see Christopher Lewis, General Books on Selection). Also a chapter called 'The Selection Interview' by Vivian Bingham in *Management Recruiting* (see above).

Testing

Toplis, J., Dulewilz, V. and Fletcher, C. *Psycholgical Testing: A Practical Guide for Employers*. Institute of Personnel Management, 1987.

A book specializing in advising its readers on psychological testing, including introducing testing in an organization, getting supplies of tests and evaluating a testing programme. Sound, practical advice for the manager on this technical area.

Equal opportunities for women

The Equal Opportunities Commission (EOC) produce a range of pamphlets on fair employment practices. The address of the EOC is in this Appendix. The pamphlets are ideal for the busy manager. They include:

Guidelines for Equal Opportunities Employers
The Sex Discrimination Act and Advertising
Fair and Efficient Selection
Avoiding Sex Bias in Selection Testing

Racial Equality

Like the EOC, the Commission for Racial Equality have a lot of useful material for employers. They have pamphlets, a regular Employment Report, and offer advice on race relations and how to eliminate racial discrimination at work. Just a few of their pamphlets are:

Equal Opportunity in Employment: A Guide for Employers
Race Relations Code of Practice
A Guide to the Race Relations Act 1976
Advertising
Employment

Reading Wider

Torrington, D. and Hall, L. *Personnel Management: A New Approach*. Prentice-Hall, 1987.

A standard work in the larger field of personnel management by a best-selling author. Aimed at the student of personnel management and the practitioner. Provides a good insight into the work of the personnel manager, with lots in it for the general manager concerned with the management of human resources. Three of its chapters are devoted to recruitment and selection.

Selection and Assessment Consultants

A few of the better-known consultants include:

Ashridge Management Development Services Ltd
Ashridge Management College
Berkhamsted
Hertfordshire HP4 1NS
Tel.: 044 284 3491

Assessment Design Services Ltd
224 Warwick Road
Kenilworth
Warwickshire CV 8 1FD
Tel.: 0926 54678

DDA
Keystone House
Boundary Road
Loudwater
High Wycombe
Bucks HP10 9PY
Tel.: 0628 810800

The Industrial Society
Peter Runge House
3 Carlton House Terrace
London SW1Y 5DG
Tel.: 01-839 4300

PA Personnel Services
Hyde Park Hosue
60a Knightsbridge
London SW1X 7LE
Tel.: 01-235 6060

Saville and Holdsworth Ltd
The Old Post House
81 High Street
Esher
Surrey KT10 9QA
Tel.: 0372 68634

Many business schools, universities and polytechnics have staff who specialize in selection and assessment and who offer consultancy. The major accounting firms offer consultancy services, as do many test suppliers.

Test Suppliers

Assessment and Selection for Employment
NFER-Nelson
Darville Hosue
2 Oxford Road East
Windsor
Berkshire SL4 1DF
Tel.: 0753 858961

Educational and Industrial Test Services Ltd
83 High Street
Hemel Hempstead
Hertfordshire HP1 3AH
Tel.: 0442 56773/68645

The Psychological Corporation Ltd
Foots Cray High Street
Sidcup
Kent DA14 5HP
Tel.: 01-300 1149

Saville and Holdsworth Ltd
The Old Post House
81 High Street
Esher
Surrey KT 10 9QA
Tel.: 0372 68634

Science Research Associates Ltd
Newton Road
Henley-on-Thames
Oxfordshire RG9 1EW
Tel.: 04912 5959

The Test Agency
Cournswood House
North Dean
High Wycombe
Buckinghamshire HP14 4NW
Tel.: 024 024 3382

Index

The Association for Management Education and Development (AMED) is the only voluntary association of professionals in the UK whose work focuses exclusively on management training, education and organization development. Membership is open to anyone involved in this significant field of work. AMED's fast growth in recent years has created a lively membership of interested people in business, government, voluntary organizations, academic institutions and managerial consultancy.

The main aim of AMED is to promote high standards of management performance so that people in organizations and communities can work with greater effectiveness. Members are therefore encouraged to meet and collaborate to improve their own professional capabilities. Activities include evening and one-day meetings, and three- to four-day events held all over the UK and in Europe. These are designed to provide members with different developmental opportunities for the various stages of their careers. They also enable members to extend their knowledge and skills, to keep in touch with frontier thinking on management, and to exchange ideas and experience.

Free publications are sent to members. These include *MEAD (Management Education and Development)*, a journal which has three issues a year and contains articles on current management training and development; frequent focus papers on topical issues; and a monthly newsletter.

For further information, contact:

AMED
Premier Hosue
77 Oxford St
London W1
01-439 1188

The Motor Makers

The Turbulent History of Britain's Car Industry

Martin Adeney

Throughout its history, British car manufacturing has proved adept at turning triumph into disaster.

From the first flush of excitement at the dawn of the motor age to the ultimate, overwhelming invasion of the foreign car, *The Motor Makers* is the most comprehensive survey of the British car industry for almost forty years. It is an entertaining and in-depth examination of how the cars we drive got to be the way they are today, from the days of the Bullnose and the Austin Seven to the fifties boom and the catastrophic slump that followed. And it is an exemplary study of great flair and greater incompetence, whose lessons remorselessly reflect upon the faults that have plagued British economic performance for the last hundred years.

'Mr Adeney has managed to take the many disparate threads spun by a complex industry over almost a century, weave them into a coherent whole and place the result in its full international context. It is no mean achievement.' *Financial Times*

'A convincing portrait of an industry more interested in takeover bids and keeping foreigners at bay than designing, making and marketing decent cars.' *Management Today*

'Fascinating.' Ian Jack, *New Statesman & Society*

FONTANA PAPERBACKS

Getting the Best Out of Yourself and Others

Buck Rodgers with Irv Levey

'A no-nonsense primer on how to succeed in business by *really* trying.' *Impact*

In *Getting the Best Out of Yourself and Others*, author of *The IBM Way*, Buck Rodgers, reveals his remarkable ability to grab people's attention, fire them with enthusiasm and move them to perform in a way they never thought possible – and he shows how you can do the same.

Writing in his engagingly warm and personal style, Buck Rodgers offers sound, practical advice on how to survive in today's fiercely competitive business world: articulating your values and beliefs, building self-esteem, improving your personal presentation, discovering the correlation between motivation and achievement, setting your own goals, connecting pay to performance, and building an atmosphere of enthusiasm at work.

If you are willing to strive towards new heights, to enhance your own capabilities and performance and maximize your potential, *Getting the Best* proves there's no limit to what you can achieve.

'It will be the rare businessman or woman who will not profit from reading [this book]. There is an abundance of common sense in this volume as well as a few very practical tips on how to put this wisdom into effect.' *New York City Tribune*

The 100 Best Companies to Work for in the UK

Bob Reynolds

Foreword by John Harvey-Jones

The 100 Best Companies to Work for in the UK is an incisive and most revealing guide to the country's key employers. From the massive multinational to the smallest family firm, these companies have one thing in common. They are all excellent employers.

In the most comprehensive survey of employment in British industry ever undertaken, more than 1500 companies have been evaluated on eight primary criteria:

- Pay
- Benefits
- Promotion
- Training
- Working Environment
- Ambience
- Equal Opportunities
- Financial Performance

A team of researchers has combed the length and breadth of the UK to find 100 excellent workplaces. See how your company performs. Rate it against the competition. Test its scale of benefits against an average top-100 best employer.

Does it match up to Marks & Spencer, which has the best pay and benefits package in the retail sector? Do its industrial relations compare with Vickers Defence Systems, which had one of the worst employment records on Tyneside a few years ago and now has one of the best? Read how staff and management achieved the turnaround.

Whether you are a company chairman, or in search of your first job, this book is essential reading. It also shows how business can boom when management offer inspired leadership and treat their employees with respect.

FONTANA PAPERBACKS